GHOSTDANCING IN VENICE

To Martin
with thanks for the
great work!

Dedicated to:

JOHN (FIRE) LAME DEER
BLACK ELK
FRANK FOOLS CROW
And all medicine men and women

GHOSTDANCING IN VENICE

George Vigileos

Engares Publishing

First published in the United Kingdom in 2007
by Engares Publishing

ISBN 978-0-9557638-0-9

Front cover: 'Birth of the Fifth Sun', by Zotec ©
Cover design and photography by Matt Brodie
Cover layout by Martin Glastonbury

Book production by The Choir Press, Gloucester
Printed and bound in Great Britain

CONTENTS

Acknowledgements

To all my dear friends, you make it all worthwhile. You are the light in this troubled world.

Special thanks to Juliet for proof reading, encouragement, and her inspirational spirit.

CHAPTER 1

FAITH

'Faith. Faith is the bridge between the mundane and the awesome, this world and the spiritual,' said Andri grabbing the table top between his thumb and his index finger to emphasise the solidity of the material level. 'Nothing's mundane in reality, it's all awesome, it's just the way we look at things that make them mundane, and faith is the bridge.'

'Faith in what?' asked Thodoras. 'That's the one which is hard to agree on, and has got people killing each other all over the planet for how many centuries now?'

'No, not belief, religion. You are talking about belief – that's another matter, all sorts of external influences there. Faith is active, it's when you move in the dark based on that which you know deep inside to be true, even if you can't see it most of the time,' said Andri. He looked outside through the bay windows on the south-western end of the house. The Sun was preparing them for the night, and the sky had erupted in rays of colour dancing around the clouds. It bothered him that the glass was dirty, although he was a student living with a group of friends in a shared house, and cleanliness was not expected, on the contrary ... but he so valued the sunlight that he didn't like being deprived of it.

'I don't know about that,' answered Thodoras, in a tone that told Andri that he would process that one in due time – maybe. He was a deep thinker, and also often a recluse in himself so it was hard to know where he was at sometimes. He rocked himself out of the deep couch and stood up to stretch. Although from Greek parents Theodoras dark skin and pitch black shoulder length hair made him look more like he was from the mountains of Peru. He had what you would describe as an average size body for a western man in his twenties, on the thin side – much like his childhood friend Andri, only with a much bigger chest – a gift from his long distance running days. 'This "journey to the inner child" stuff here is quite interesting,' he said holding up some academic journal. 'What do you think of that?'

'Hmm. Childhood, yes. Actions packed with symbolism. I think that reality at the level we are living at is highly symbolic. We act in a certain way that is designed to bring about the issues we need to deal with, and hopefully to learn the lessons we need. But at another level our actions can be like an eternal dance. For example, childhood takes us through the same stages as has the development of humanity, the changes in consciousness, it takes us through what humanity as a whole has achieved so far,' said Andri rubbing his chin.

'Did you say achieved? Wrong word. More what we didn't achieve. To be human,' said Thodoras.

'True' conceded Andri. 'But you must agree, there is a developmental parallel here. Its root, I think, is from the time consciousness was more tied into the tribe, the clan, whatever. When humans were still deeply connected with the Earth. Before we forgot, before the fall. Once we realised individual consciousness, we started our hopeless effort to divorce ourselves from our own nature. But deep inside we're still connected, and we go through the motions – the acting out the changes of consciousness of the human animal in our own childhood development. All in a nutshell, but strangely most of the time we live our lives without recalling why we do what we do. It never ceases to amaze me how much is hidden so close to our eyes,' said Andri glancing at Thodoras who was lying back with his eyes shut, showing no signs of life. 'Lost you? Happens to me all the time, story of my life! Anyway, to answer your question, I don't remember much of my early childhood. We lived in Madrid, in a neighbourhood which was then at the edge of the city. I vaguely recall playing with the gypsy kids that lived on the hill.'

CHAPTER 2

THE GYPSY'S STORY

'Ouch!' exclaimed Andri putting his right hand on the top of his head. There was blood pouring down his cheek and dripping onto his cotton t-shirt.

'I'll get the bastard!' he thought to himself. The others had long gone down the hill, leaving him there to hold the enemy off. One last sniper on the enemy side had got the best of him. He peeked out of his fox hole. Nobody there to be seen. He took a better look. Nothing.

'He must have thrown the last stone right before he left,' he thought. It was getting late, almost dusk, and he should be heading home before his folks started looking for him. Being five wasn't all fun and games and being good for mommy. The ongoing war with the gypsy kids from the camp on top of the hill was serious business. The hillside was a right battlefield, steps carved out of the hard soil on the steep side, and foxholes on the way up the smooth approach.

'We did our best to hold them off again,' he thought. 'Maybe I can still catch up with the sniper and have a last say. Yes, I will!' Andri made a mad dash across no-man's land, to the safety of the big rocks on the gypsy side. Slowly around, and another quick dash to the left, hidden by the tall grass. He could see the edge of the gypsy camp now, the first caravans! His heart was pounding fast, never been so close to the enemy's stronghold before. What an adventure, his friends would regret missing this! Driven by some mad idea of getting to the enemy's camp, and the rush of curiosity that was egging him on he found himself under a caravan looking from behind a big wooden wheel. There was a fire in the middle of the camp, which looked more like a village from where he was crouching. The deep orange flames of the fire seemed to be dancing even before the hand struck the guitar strings. The player was a gypsy man in his thirties. He was wearing green bell trousers, a black shirt, dark yellow waistcoat, and a grey scarf full of sequins. As he bowed his head over the guitar neck he seemed to smirk under his dark moustache. He yelled to a little boy who quickly ran to his side – whispered something in his ear and kept on playing some warm tunes. Andri's eyes focused back on the guitar. The music was sweet and melodic, almost putting him into a trance. Suddenly, the little boy had sprouted in front of his face on the other side of the wooden cart wheel spokes and was pointing at him excitedly. A much older boy appeared next to him and grabbed him by the arm.

'Hey, let go!' Andri protested as the two boys dragged him in front of the player.

'And who is this little mouse who thinks he's gonna sneak up to our camp? And what shall we do with him, roast him on the fire and have him for supper?'

The crowd of gypsies who had gathered around the fire roared in laughter.

Andri's heart sank. He was desperately hoping that all the stories the grown-ups told about the gypsies were lies, made up to scare the children, like the bad witch. Maybe he could escape now that they were all laughing. He tried to pull himself loose from the older boy, but failed as the grip on his arm tightened. 'Ouch! Let me go!' he wailed in protest, in hope.

'Bring the lad here!' The voice was full of authority, and the face of the old crone where it came from spoke of many years and much wisdom. It was quickly obeyed, and Andri found himself almost shepherded to the old woman's large blue skirt.

'Let me see you now,' she said as she carefully took his left hand and looked at it. She almost straightened herself upright suddenly, and then bent forward to take a good look in his eyes. 'Why, he's a raven child! Just like us, but from a different fire,' she said in a deep raspy voice.

Strangely, he felt a comfort when she looked at him, a feeling of the sea gently rocking a small boat in the moonlight. Her face had a strange quality, dark skin and pretty features, which however seemed to float on her face, yet he could tell she must have been very pretty once. He looked up to the sky behind her and noticed it was getting dark now, and the first stars had shown themselves. He loved this time of day. He knew somewhere in his brain that he should be heading home, that he would be missed already, and yet he felt quite at home where he was.

'Stay a while and I'll tell you a story,' said the crone, as if reading the worry in his mind. He looked at her deep brown eyes, then squat on the ground resting his back on the big smooth log she was sitting on, and listened. In front of him the flames were now a deep orange colour, throwing off tiny white sparks from the edges, like the stars that were now shimmering all over the dark blue sky.

'Once upon a time, long, long, long ago, there was a big city. All the houses were low and made of clay, and in the middle stood palaces and temples, made of stone and pointing to the sky. Back then the priests, well they had real powers because they had found out some of the secrets of the Earth, and could read the messages from the stars. The kings and priests however became very greedy, and wouldn't share their powers with people, instead used them to control them. The people became more and more poor, and had to work harder and harder whilst the nasty kings and priests adorned their palaces and temples with gold and precious stones.

Soon the Earth started rumbling and complaining about these goings on, the clouds brought no rain, and in the fields the crops were failing. The grown-ups did not know what to do, they were always tired and hungry and couldn't think straight anymore.

So the children got together in secret at night, and decided to send one of them to the mountain, to ask the sky for his help. And so they chose for a boy called Aeeneean to go. His parents had vanished in the temples one night, never to be seen again. He lived rough on his own, so he wouldn't be missed by anyone. The children met the next night and gave Aeeneean a bundle to take with him for the journey. He also brought his knife, a pair of flint stones in a small beaded bag his grandmother had made for him, and a small blanket. He quietly strapped it all on his body and left for the mountains.

He had hardly left the cultivated fields headed for the hills when he met an old man by the side of the path. 'I'm hungry,' said the old man hardly able to speak he was so weak. 'Can you give me something to eat?' he asked. Aeeneean looked in his bag and found a small loaf of bread and some cheese. He handed them over to the old man and went to set off again, when the old man stopped him. 'Where are you headed to?' he asked.

'To the top of the mountains, so I can ask Grandfather Sky to help us, for the king and his priests have become greedy and are starving us to death.' The old man reached out and in his hand he put a stone.

'This will help you on your way,' he said, and then he turned into a crow and flew away. Aeeneean kept going up the hills and into the deep forest at the foot of the big mountain. There he ran into a bear who had been snared by a hunter's trap and was hanging from its leg off a tall tree branch. To his surprise the bear spoke to him, and said:

'Please help me, get me down, and I will not harm you.' Aeeneean, although he was very scared of the big ferocious animal, realised it must be a sacred spirit, because it talked to him and he understood it. So he took his knife out of its sheath and cut it down. The bear then pulled out its longest strongest claw from its front right foot and gave it to him saying 'This will help you get there,' and it vanished in the mist.

Aeeneean kept going through the forest until he reached the stream at the edge of the trees. There, as he went to get some water as he was thirsty from the walk, he met a lizard. It stood still as a rock, and he touched it to make sure it wasn't dead, when the lizard said to him:

'Oh, please little boy, I am but a small lizard but the sun has been hiding from me, and I am frozen to the bone. Can you please warm me up?'

So Aeeneean build a fire with his flints and warmed the lizard up so he revived.

'I would be forever grateful to you,' he said, 'if you could find it in your heart to give me those flints so I can always stay warm.'

Aeeneean realised that again this must be a sacred spirit talking to him, so he gave the flints to the lizard and moved on to climb the mountain. Soon it was night time again, and he stopped to rest. He was hungry and cold, without food or flint to make a fire, so he wrapped himself in his blanket, and as he was very tired he quickly fell asleep.'

The old crone paused for a moment as she stirred the tobacco in her pipe with her long black fingernail. As she sucked on the pipe the camp fire lit up stronger. Andri's eyes focused temporarily on the two young dancers swirling around each other as the flames roared. Part of the old crone's shawl was wrapped around his shoulders, her hand gently caressing his hair, as she continued with the story.

'In his dream, Aeeneean saw a green dragon. It roared and spat fire from its huge mouth and said, 'Give me all your food, or I will eat you up!'

Aeeneean reached into his bag for the food, and instead he felt the stone. He remembered the old man who was a crow and he threw the stone at the dragon's open mouth who exploded into a big fireball and disappeared. Aeeneean woke up and was surprised to find out that by his feet was a fire. It snowed then, only it was no ordinary snow, it was like white corn. So he ate the white corn and warmed his body by the fire.

In the morning, he headed off to climb the steepest part of the mountain, through the clouds where the rock was almost bare. As he climbed he got to a big rock he could not climb anymore, because the fire had made it too tall and the wind too smooth. So he remembered the claw the bear had given him, and he used it to climb the big rock. When he got to the top he thanked the crow, the lizard and the bear for their help, and the Earth and Sky for sending them to him. He then opened his arms to the heavens above and sang a song which said:

'Grandfather Sky, the children have sent me to ask you to help us. The people are suffering and we have no power, for the king and the priests have taken it and hidden it from us. The rains haven't come for a long time now, and the Earth will bear its fruit no more. So they sent me to tell you, and to ask you to help us, for we are your children too.'

And the Sky was so touched by the little child's song that his heart opened and out fell a star. The star was huge but the Sky put it in the palm of his hand and squeezed it into the smallest and most beautiful light. This he gave to the boy and said in a thunderous whisper:

'Swallow this star, and go back to the people, and when the time is right it will help you all to be free.'

'But Grandfather, how will I know when the time is right?' asked Aeeneean.

'Every night look at the stars in me, and when the time is right I will move them from their place and then you will know.'

Aeeneean swallowed the star and felt its warmth in his belly. He thanked Father Sky and then headed down the mountain. He climbed down the rock face of the peak with renewed courage and a lightness in his heart. He couldn't wait to get back to his people and tell them the good news.

On the way down the mountain, just inside the first trees where the green carpet hugs the towering stone peaks a large dark figure moved. Its eyes – fires – like stars reflecting off the surface of a lake, black as the night, looking straight at him – left leg barely touching the ground – poised to move. Aeeneean froze to the spot. A shiver ran down his spine and he struggled to keep from shaking. He felt like running but knew well that the massive black jaguar could pounce on him if it wanted to and he wouldn't even have made it to the trees. Instead, it turned its head and looked straight at him with amazing warmth and empathy. He dropped to the ground as his knees involuntarily buckled in relief. He looked again at the trees, lifting his head slightly. The jaguar had vanished. He lay on his back for a while looking at the trees, the clouds slowly drifting over a light blue sky. A raven dropped through the air like a rock, swooping at the last moment to fly just over the tree tops.

For the next few days as he journeyed down the mountains and through the dense jungle towards the village he felt the presence of the jaguar, as if it was always close to him but just out of sight. It was a reassuring feeling, one of companionship with a gentle but powerful spirit.'

'So what happened after all that?' asked Andri.

'When the time came around and all was ready – long after the children of his children's children had passed over to be with the ancestors, Grandfather Sky moved and made the stars shift. Then Aeeneean stood amidst his people, and the star came out of the top of his head. Its white blue light was so strong and beautiful, that the king and the priests knew their time had come, and fled. They got on their boats and paddled furiously to get away, but the river snapped its tail, twisted its huge head around and devoured them. Then the star sank into the Earth, and where it went in a Tree came out, the likes of which had not be seen for many generations. And seeing the Tree, Grandfather Sky was so happy that tears ran off his face, and the Earth turned green and bountiful once again. And the people rejoiced holding hands in a big circle around the tree and sang and danced to thank the Sky and the Earth for their freedom.'

'And now I've told you the story and it has been told.' As she said this, the old crone reached her arm out to the sky and then gently nudged Andri off the log. Time for you to go home now, before your parents show up with the police, go on, off you go.'

Andri started back begrudgingly, the story still twisting in his mind.

The old crone signalled to a little gypsy boy, slingshot ready. The stone flew over the night sky and landed right on Andri's head. He stumbled and fell over. A moment later he was feeling his head with his right hand. 'Ouch!' he said more in surprise rather than in pain. His head was bleeding. He looked up amazed that it was so dark already. Only a moment ago he was chasing the last sniper, and it was still daytime.

'I must have passed out' he thought. He could hear his mother's voice from a distance looking for him. 'I'm in trouble now,' he thought to himself as he got out of the foxhole and headed to the bright electric lights of the big apartment buildings at the edge of the hillside . . .

Andri knew he had a special relationship with stones early on in life. When his father, an accomplished engineer who had worked on hydroelectric dams all over the world talked to him about geology on their excursions in the countryside, he would listen with fascination about the tremendous forces that shape the earth, and how the rocks were formed through fire or water. He liked picking up stones and rubbing them with his fingers, and looking at them all around. Sometimes he'd pick one and carry it around and find another home for it, or even take it home in his pocket. The stones would communicate with him, not in voice like animals do, but in a secret language he knew well and could sense through his bones. Later in life, even when all other faith had gone, he would still go and 'listen' to the pebbles on the beach, for they are in touch with the great oceans and know much about what is about to unfold.

CHAPTER 3
KNOW YOURSELF

'This is exactly what I mean. I've told you something about yourself, for the second time now, and you can't even let yourself hear it!' Vincent was almost shouting at Andri to manage to be heard above the noisy clutter of his mind. They were standing in the corridor outside the bathroom on the third floor of the old wooden house in Boston where they all lived together. There were a few of them around tripping on acid, and the air was thick with colourful energy vibrations. The corridor turned ninety degrees behind Andri, leading to a couple of bedroom doors on the one side, one on the other, and ending in the living room – a long room with a bay of windows on the far end looking out to the small garden and the street. The other end of the corridor led to the kitchen, and through that to another bedroom, with sash windows looking towards the city, and again toward the garden, which consisted mainly of one huge maple tree around which the house was seemingly built. The tree was tall enough to lay its top branches on top of the flat roof of the house.

From one of the bedrooms behind him he could hear Thodoras, trying desperately to explain on the phone something of his profound life altering realisations to his mother, of all people to be talking to when on a trip! His wandering consciousness was abruptly re-focused when Vincent brushed past him in frustration, almost knocking him over. Yet, even at the slow pace of the moment unravelling then sinking in, he knew Vincent was right. He was well aware of the existence of shadows in his soul, where he hid things from himself – as we all do. He knew that the moment was there to remind him forever of the blindness and deafness of the soul that lives in fear, and the immense difficulty of the task in hand – to know one's self. Oh yes, the master of illusions is the self, and it will go to great lengths to survive – knowing well that inevitably it's there to be transcended. Yes, Andri had read the old philosophy books, the wisdom of so many distilled into so few core instructions for spiritual growth, and had concluded that beyond doubt to know your self was one of the most fundamental and essential ones. And yet, the self is elusive, and spiritual mirrors are hard to come by – so much easier to live in deception. So we do.

The Spring Street group were all eager to learn from each other, open to infinite possibilities, especially those where life was good! The good energy wanted to come out to share itself. So soon enough, they were having great change of the season parties, and every equinox and solstice people would gather. There were hundreds of people coming to these parties, word of mouth took care of that, and the revival of arts, spirituality, music and all that rock and roll vibration about the place kept it all mostly good. Even the cops didn't bother them too much, to the dismay of some of their neighbours, and who could blame them? Two live bands, plus a trance drum percussion room, all together with the dancing and bopping, the drunk joviality and all that goes with such a hootenanny four times a year can become too much at 4am. Still, the parties kept going! And the rest of the time, well it was at least the sounds of rock and roll blasting through the speakers or the house band, which consisted of a few aspiring regulars plus who ever happened to be there at the time, resulting in some inspired moments, consistently inconsistent.

☯

For Thodoras and Andri, the two Greeks, things were a bit different. Due to being brought up in more outright dictatorships, they were a bit like babes in the woods. New to drugs and all that, they had a different perspective on things, as their introduction to psychedelics happened at a time they were ready to search in those realms, more purposeful and focused than if they had been turned on to them as kids. They had a distinct readiness to deal with what they saw. And so it was, and it came to be an influence on the whole dynamics of the group. Life was on a nice balance as they worked and learned, danced and played, created and absorbed. Life was full, full of people, energy, activity.

Even the most seeming inactive day was full of newness and vibrations. People were in and out of relationships, or in more long term ones, so there was always dramatic variety in the social scene and that was ok too. Anything seemingly constant would rarely be there by the next season, apart from the good stuff. That's not to say there were no bad times, the lessons in life are ever present. It's when we don't learn from them that they come back again and again.

Back in those days, where everything was about exploration and discovery, breaking new ground and reconnecting with ancient wisdom, time had a different quality. Sometimes it blew by with the force of a strong wind, other times it seemed to almost come to a standstill, but most of the time it flowed like maple syrup on a hot pancake. It was one of those syrupy summer days. James was carving a piece of red cedar, a broken shingle from a job the gang were doing outside Boston. Being an avid woodsman and carpenter, James had a special relationship with the wood, and as a constant reminder his long matted blond hair and beard seemed to be a permanent host to assorted wood chippings. On the one side of the shingle he carved a Sun, strong and warm and full of energy. Inside the Sun he carved a crescent moon and a star. On the other side just one word: 'breathe'.

Some days were wrapped up in mist, like the breath of a huge dragon, rhythmical and full of magic. Like the day when Thomas walked in. The group had gathered to interview people for the one room that had become available when Edward moved out – headed west, back to his folks. It was a small room, but central, and anyway they were all quite aware of the special energy that was building up, so it was important to find the right character. They were all gathered around the wooden table in the kitchen on the third floor, two weather beaten sash windows letting the late morning light in. The table was as always hosting coffee and beer mugs, ashtrays and newspapers, all the normal student fare. Strangely there were always interesting books floating about as well, mostly on the topics of religion, spirituality and politics, as you would expect of a bunch of theology students! Apart from Andri that is. He was then studying economic development, partly because the influences in his life, partly chance, partly his interest in some notion of socio-economic fairness and his communist past. Still, he had a vested interest in studying spiritual stuff, it just kept popping up in his life regardless, so at some level it was more than just addressing a curiosity. He felt a thirst for matters of the Spirit, a yearning for more light to be shed on the path he clearly felt he was on.

They had already interviewed a couple of people, nice enough, possible roommates, maybe. Then Thomas walked in. When this happened and he introduced himself, the air took that liquid quality, which Andri had experienced before as what most people would generally categorise as 'a spiritual experience'.

'That is only before a soul starts living from that space, because when truly centred it becomes clear that reality is much more that than this and more this than that!' he thought to himself. The atmosphere became instantly familiar, so much that with almost only non verbal communication they had already decided to take him on. What Thomas said as a consequence, was something like

'... and you will find yourself with a group of good hearted people, in some sort of cosmic elevator – going up!' The feeling of total deja vu permeated the meeting. The kitchen, with its warped wooden floors, sagging in the middle from the memories of many wild pagan parties, was magically transformed into the galley of a pirate ship, har har me maties and a bottle of rum type. Hardly surprising as they were in Boston, and the coast here was well acquainted to the creaky sails and rough rumblings of smugglers and pirates. Andri took it as a good sign, and things moved on. He stored it somewhere in there in the good feeling file with a question mark as to its deeper meaning. His thinking on such experiences had mostly been that it would be very hard indeed to distinguish an experience triggered by a place as it could be either a memory held by the place itself, or a person that used to live in that time period. Whether the person who experiences this time travel is tuning in to another person from the past or whether in some form the person or an ancestor of this person was there it is hard to discern. In deed, the mere fact that most westerners who believe in reincarnation imagine themselves as having been some King, Queen, powerful witch or wizard and rarely a slave scrubbing the floor, or piss bucket carrier for the royalty, led him to believe that the bias of wishful thinking plays an important role in their belief ... However these experiences are, and in his mind they beckoned investigation, for they were not random but purposeful.

So too was what Thomas said that day. Later on as he was moving some of his stuff in, he pulled out a poster that was sticking out of a box of books and laid it on the kitchen table. It was a poster advertising a theatre festival in Venice. The actors were dressed in the traditional festival outfits, as jugglers and conjurers, costumes from the days when Venice ruled the Mediterranean, when the people feared the state more than the pirates, who for the most part were just entrepreneurs inclined to carve out their own niche, literally. The poster sent Andri off again. He had this strong feeling that it was important, that he should remember it. Venice, theatre, something. He started thinking that maybe, since his parents both came from an island which was under the Venetians for many years, there could be a blood connection, something in his ancestral past that rang a bell.

'Something to look into, surely,' he muttered.

'What are you muttering about again amigo?' asked Thodoras, inviting him to the living room. Andri stepped away from his bedroom door and sat on the light brown couch, fumbling on the coffee table for something to smoke.

'I don't quite know ... it's this feeling of déjà vu. One picture of a place in the past and I find myself transported to another world. A world I somehow know intimately, a place in space and time of which I have specific emotional memories. What gets me is that it's not random, it feels very strongly that there's a purpose, a specific reason why I am remembering.' Andri paused and cupped his hands over his eyes and then moved them to the back of his neck.

'Hmm, yes, I know the feeling ... something more than just fishing in the collective unconscious. The key is the purpose of course ...' Thodoras looked up and put his fingers together in a characteristic eastern fashion.

'Imagine though, if you had a deeper memory and could remember enough of your past lives to make use of your experience ... but you know, it just occurred to me that we do – when we die. Sure, from a place of living in spirit, which presumably is what happens when we die, we could string together our lives, again if that's what happens ... we might be aware enough to design not one but many lifetimes as one journey ... Wow! The possibilities are then endless!' Andri almost jumped out of his seat in the realisation of what he was saying.

'Satori!' exclaimed Thodoras. 'I like the sound of that! It means that, hopefully, some day we'll wake up to discover that life is perfect, happening just as it should, cause that is the film we dreamed of. It also fits in a way with this stuff coming out of quantum physics, you know all that about there being parallel universes and such.'

'Funny you should mention that ...' said Andri after a brief pause. 'I've been thinking of parallel universes, I mean you run into it all the time in science fiction books, it has almost become a common literary tool used to intertwine two or more stories together. It's had me thinking, this concept. There's something there ...'

'Well, there's two ways to look at it. Either there are two universes happening at the same time, like two rooms in the same house the one alternative to the other in some way. Or, they exist at different times, past and future leaking into the present. That would explain some elements of déjà vu I suppose,' replied Thodoras.

'And a third possibility, that both you mentioned are true. In any case, I wonder if and how these worlds affect each other. They must, come to think of it, nothing is without connection to everything else, and I can imagine that parallel universes would have many such connections to each other ... windows to another world.' Andri got up and walked to the big bay window overlooking the busy avenue at the bottom of the street. He looked out into the setting Sun.

CHAPTER 4

A WEDDING IN VENICE

I saw a man with a black side and a red side, braids on the black side and loose hair on the red ... The loose hair was there for sorrow, so that they could wipe their tears as those who lament in the Sun Dance. The man wore buckskin leggings, quillwork, and three rows of eagle claws around his neck and was carrying a pipe. He had the most beautiful outfit I had ever seen. The man said: "When you conduct meetings to heal, I will be there."[1]

-DAWSON NO HORSE-

Venice, early 1500s

'Tomaso, draw the curtains please, I feel there's someone looking in on us.'

'I see no one out there Guisepe ...' replied Tomaso in a low tone, almost a whisper. He could feel it himself oddly enough, although the anticipation of rehearsal day had made him edgy. Now that the sun was setting and they were all in the cabin in the woods he felt much safer. He pulled the dark cloth over the small window as someone lit a candle. He couldn't make out any details of people's

faces in the dim light, but he knew everyone was present; magic circles tend to be that way. Franco's voice boomed in the pregnant silence.

'Make no mistake my friends – fellow conspirators, making yourself invisible takes lots of practice, just like any other important skill.' Franco was organising the training groups, and leaving no illusions in their minds, '... and as my old friend the wizard used to say, there's no substitute for doing the thing itself, best pray and jump in, keep focused on absolute faith or face the consequences.'

Although the old building was well out of the way and quite safe, people stirred around nervously. Nobody in there wanted particularly to be reminded of the consequences. The tortures routinely going on in the dark palace cells were enough to focus the mind on not getting caught alive, not to mention the 'special' treatment reserved for anyone plotting against the monarch – wrapping your guts around your neck would be merciful in comparison! And now, they were all rehearsing prancing and dancing around the guards, performing their own act, '... because even guards have memories, and a good implant will make things look more normal during the event itself. We will run it through up to the point of final action, and then disband and melt away, just as on the day of the wedding – nothing will go wrong, don't worry its counterproductive, no, its down right risky!' said Giusepe.

Giusepe was central to the planning process, and had gone to many lengths to get as clear a vision on events as possible, identifying – as he put it – the one potential strand of actions out of infinite possible, that will lead to the future they desire. Still, the plot didn't make any apparent sense – and when Thomaso had pointed that out at the first meeting Giusepe insisted that it was this central feature which made it safe, as it was beyond the logic of the established powers, and yet in harmony with the divine plan that brought them together in the first place.

The next morning, a group of street entertainers danced their way on the fringes of St. Mark's square. Security was extra tight, in preparation for the dress rehearsal for the big wedding, and there were two very different rehearsals going on.

'Why on Earth are we taking such a huge risk, to be spotted by the guards and it isn't even the day, the Doge won't even appear for the dress rehearsal! So pray explain to me what this is all about!' Thomaso, dressed in his green and yellow jester costume knew the answer well before he finished the question ... it had all seemed so clear in his mind when Franco had explained it in his usual matter of fact way, of how all the old shamans have always used such techniques in times of need. They had all taken turns to mill around the high risk areas which they would normally go to great lengths to avoid, where the guards had a good view and easy control of possible escape routes.

Thomaso didn't necessarily always share Guisepe's strength of faith, but he knew well that this was the wrong time for doubt, and he quickly proceeded to meditate the thought out of his head. It always amazed him when he got back into the flow of the group how clearly he crossed that boundary, and just in time as it turned out. A guard had started to focus on him dangerously, and now seemed to distract himself, his eyes starting to wander off again.

'That was close!' he murmured under his breath to reassure himself. He could feel the others moving through the crowds, aimlessly yet in a tight pattern, in your face yet invisible. Soon the group had paraded in sequence in front of the bemused guards standing in front of the side entrance to the cathedral's basement, long ago abandoned and sealed after the collapse years ago which killed a team of sanitation workers trapping rats during the days of the black death. Their bodies had been left there, and no one in their right mind would even think of venturing in such a death trap, another reason why the plan made no sense! The door was rusted shut anyway, and even if they managed to break the lock there was no guarantee that they would be able to get to the main chamber – right under the altar and the steps where the royal couple would stand. No guarantee apart from the fact that most of them had experienced visions or dreams finding themselves under there, performing their own little wedding. That was of course the other big shocker, that they were planning all this, not to actually kill the Doge, using a good amount of dynamite for example – which would be the thing revolutionaries do – but to destroy the ruling elite's power, reclaiming the power for all the people. All this to be achieved through magic ritual, a symbolic performance of the spiritual wedding of opposing inner forces, the letting loose of the two serpents and making whole that which a long time ago the Doges of this world separated – the people from their power. The mystical union of the Earth and the Sky, that will give birth to the good future, and as Guisepe had said: 'Even if we don't live to see it this time around – it will be a key piece of reality for the future generations to tap into – when the last act will be played out for humanity.'

Of course there was no point asking why they couldn't do all this in the dark woods, where they usually practised ritual, in the safety of nature's bosom, or why they had to do it at the same time the damn Doge was getting married, and the main plaza would be full of soldiers – looking out for rebels like themselves. Only they weren't rebels, they were, how did Felipe put it, proponents of a deeper reality, actors for the manifestation of the divine will, which can only be based on love and understanding. Yes, the safety catch, the ultimate scales to judge anything by. If there's not enough love going around it is because we are given a free will, and so many just don't will love beyond the self serving romantic kind, just enough to keep the physical body alive, but completely disregard the needs of the soul, the inevitability of the spirit.

By now the group had mostly dispersed, drifting down the narrow alleys which branched off the four main bridges to the square. There was to be no meeting tonight, everybody was to go about their own lives keeping in touch only when necessary for the next week, until the day itself arrived. This was a crucial time, and very dangerous, as the impending action creates its own trace in the dream world, traces that some are keenly looking for, for the Doge has his own wizards working overtime, and many other eyes and ears around feeling for any unfamiliar bits of information floating about.

Yet, there was a sense of relaxation – the familiar ease with which things tend to happen after a tense and demanding undertaking, such as the dress rehearsal. The mind wanders, familiar patterns emerge, and the soul beckons for some entertainment, the body for some refreshment. Thomaso found himself sipping a mug of warm wine, watching the prostitutes laughing and carousing with the less than dignified clientele of the Fat Boar. 'The hell with solitude and prayer, I could well be dead or worse next week! I'm getting laid tonight, I need my own body happy. Anyway, what harm could it do?' Another mug full later he was quietly disappearing down the corridor, embraced with a red head woman, unnoticed to all but a pair of familiar eyes glancing from behind the bar. Jesobell, the proprietor's pretty daughter was still watching him when a second figure, Bruno Carroti, a well known henchman with a nasty reputation for slitting people's throat for no apparent reason, followed purposefully behind.

☯

Giusepe was drawing himself together after a routine scan of the energies floating around the cottage and the surrounding woods by the hills when he was alerted by what seemed like a dark bird flying straight at him. It was a raven carrying an owl's feather in its talons. A sure sign of trouble, something was wrong; one of the group members was in danger. He picked his coat and swiftly made his way through the trees to the town's edge, heading for the meeting place by the cemetery. Franco was already there, pacing about.

'Jesobell from the Fat Boar came over, I think Thomaso's in trouble – we must act quickly!' Franco's voice was calm and tense at the same time reflecting his inner struggle to 'keep the energy pool from rippling too much,' well aware that at some level of existence, excitement can be sensed by the trained mind.

As Franco talked about what had happened, the scenario started piling up in Giusepe's mind. Thomaso was a known risk, after all he used to be a monk in this area years ago, and as he pointed out when they had first met, local monasteries are a great place to do all sorts of inner work, and also to meet others – many of which are failed politicians – even ex-doges! His usefulness as part of the group were thus obvious from the start, so too was the risk presented by those same connections. The men of the Dieci – the council of ten which effectively took over power from the Doges after the failed revolution of 1310 – were as nasty a secret police as any, and they would certainly be looking out for people with connections to the monasteries. After all, the monasteries, protected by the church were a highly likely nest for conspirators. So they had an eye out for him, and he went to town – to drink, to hide his fear in a mug and the warmth of a woman. An ex-monk in such a sinners den. Maybe he could get away with it though, although his lack of history there would make his situation more obvious, there's always a first time, a fall from grace. Yes, the possible route to a good resolution was starting to form more clearly. Now, to change some mindsets around.

Carroti was ready to pounce, when the two stormed into the room. Thomaso would have died a quiet death, completely unaware of the killer's blade already drawn under his cloak, now wavering in stunned disbelief, the hyena denied the kill! 'You whore! How dare you!' Giusepe was explaining to the stunned Bruno very quickly about how the redhead's father – Franco in the lead role performing for everyone's life – was enraged and would deal with her, and lover boy, with great pain involved for both. Something about a good family friends of the Doge and avoiding a scandal, your services will be remembered none the less, and the villan's knife made its way back to the sheath. In the meantime, Franco had shepherded the other two outside, and soon all were gone in the cold damp night. After the girl was escorted to a safe place and convinced to forget about it all with a gold coin in her hand, to remind her to forget as Franco put it half menacing, the three friends headed for the little house in the woods.

☯

The air was misty, heavy – full of water a good conduit to slip in and disappear. Instinctively and without a word, the three friends took separate paths and vanished in the shadows of the night, just in case anyone had managed to tag along. Soon, Giusepe was feeling the water from his own sweat on his skin just as much as that in the air, he felt like he was almost swimming ... The heavy robe was dragging him down now, had served its purpose and had to go. He knew where this was going, kind of. He knew he was moving into another place, as he kept on taking his clothes off and letting them drop on the forest floor, some little voice inside taking note for later and also scolding himself, but this outburst of spirit living the vision could not be stopped, the inner commitment was already offered. Slowly, letting go drifting into a dream-like reality.

Bare feet now on the moist forest floor, water streaming off his chest as he found himself running, naked, feeling the earth with his feet, the sounds of birdsong in his head, an image of the tribal fire on the high plains, the feeling of the tribe sitting around the fire. 'I am the tribe – the tribe is me – we are one' echoed in his head as he ran faster, his feet deeper in the earth, losing himself as he came to a clearing, sinking in the quicksand, his vision focused on a white limestone throne at the edge of the trees, on which lay an empty snail's shell and a white flower, glowing.

When he came to, he realised that – still in a daze – he had backtracked, picked up his clothes and taken his body over to the pine trees. His heart was still pounding from the excitement, and he almost felt sick to his stomach as if hitting land after a lengthy journey in the stormy sea. Well, in a way it was very much like that. After all, wow! The realisation of the significance of that vision at this junction in time just struck him, like a bolt of lightning through a clear blue sky. The vision was a message, about a link between this life and another, this state of consciousness and an ancient one, but it was as if he knew back then what he does now, a strong feeling of mystery, awe inspiring mystery! Wow! It was that feeling, which he could still recall and now had come to identify more, that quality of the light that lets you know that what you are experiencing is not only true, but of a deeper reality, so deep that we can only get a glimpse of it through symbols, stories, visions. Yet these have always been available, from the beginning, and the experience of the Spirit, the mystical alchemical union ... so beyond space and time that it seems unchanging whilst continually in motion. 'The paradox fortifies the logic!' he thought to himself.

☯

More present now, Giusepe felt strangely drawn towards the meeting place, the old barn. Strangely, because they had all agreed to stay away from there and to disband until the day itself, so as not risk detection by the secret police. The feeling was persistent, beckoning, so he went along with it, not surprised to find out as he got there that the whole group was gathered, all apparently being pulled by the same force.

'Well, since we are all here, in spite of ourselves, then we are meant to be here..' started Felipe, who liked exploring the obvious as much as he liked the 'far out there stuff' as he often put it. 'I couldn't put it better myself!' shouted Franco, as everyone chuckled. Well almost everyone; Thomaso was standing in the corner, his stance betraying his feelings of guilt in spite of his promise to himself 'never to have to feel that horrible feeling ever again!' as he announced not long ago, on one of those jovial celebratory occasions.

‘A coincidence that cannot just be has occurred again I have to tell you about it …’ Giusepe was always apprehensive of talking about a recent vision, even to this crowd, partly because it was a sign of respect to the Spirit to let things sink in, and also because some details important to trigger the understanding of the vision might not have shown themselves to the eyes yet. This time however, there was no denying the immediate connection of the vision with another part of their plans, an action of deep faith – the rendezvous.

Giusepe proceeded to describe his vision, the tribal mind consciousness humans had developed, and the transformation to individual consciousness. The symbolism of the one shell on top of the throne made of the stone which is made of myriad shells, the collective mind and the individual. All part of the spiritual evolution we have to undertake in order to better understand and closer feel the Spirit which moves in all things, the Creator. Just as the flower unfolds each petal to feel the divine light from every angle it possibly can, so we too unfold to experience more and more of the Great Mystery, which although infinite, all encompassing and forever, has given to each and every being the ability to feel its essence directly through what we call love.

It seemed like such a long shot, but the logic had it, that much was clear.

‘The possibility in this case points to a path which when undertaken leads to the inevitable. In other words, since we can conceive of it as possibly happening it is certain that it will, will being the key – our will, our decision to commit and the power of the Will of God to actually carry it through. Who can argue on that?' said Guisepe with confidence. But all the rest of them did want to argue about it as it turned out, 'till the early hours! After all, they all knew of the Fraticelli, and about the massacre in southern France in their grandfather's times, the risk of what they were already doing was immense, a network of villages, free in mind and spirit, mostly right under the church's nose. And then there were the truly free communities, hidden out there in the seas, a real thorn in the side of the established order of things. The risks were piling up, and although that may be inevitable it was not good.

Yet, at the end, they all agreed that it must be and so it shall be. A rendezvous in a few hundred years – exact date to be established by the course of events, in another significant place on the Earth – exact location to be determined by the conditions needed and thus provided. That is to say if there was anything left of any one of them by then in any shape or form, which could remember somewhere deep inside what this was all about. A group formed and bound to facilitate with the transitions of humanity. After all, they had been brought together this time around, a healing magic circle, the esoterics with a good heart. From all religions and traditions and beyond came their tools, from the lives of many before them the teachings of the medicine. Surely then, in some form, they could return to help again. It would make sense that the meeting would happen close to the big change, the end of this age as many of the old ones have talked about.

'So, in case we do meet again, how will we know? What will trigger the remembrance? A key? A symbol?' asked Franco.

'No, nothing so visible. Sure, symbols appear in our lives, and they do reveal their true meaning to us, when we are ready to see them. But that's stuff in everyone's path and can mean various things, all sorts of lessons to be learnt. No, the remembrance will come through a story, a story about this all, about us and this trip. Mind you, there will be many stories out there, and some very similar to this one, as there are many circles even within one nation – one tribe. So therefore, it has to be specific, right on to be of use to us in particular, and general enough to be of use to all else who read it – after all a story is a story!'

'Woe, hold on a minute! We could all be all over the globe, and a story will connect us all just like that?! Smells of foolish arrogance to me!' said Felipe.

'Sure, you could be right. Let's look at this together,' said Guisepe honestly. 'We've established that it is possible that we could meet hundreds perhaps years from now, to help our fellow humans and all our relations to move into the next age, a higher state of consciousness. That since this thought occurred to us, it could be that other circles could also be thinking the same thing. And, in any case, as it is the nature of esoteric mysticism to keep the wisdom alive for humanity to heal, many similar stories already exist. And all the good stories are good and have a positive effect on the whole. Yet we are talking about something more specific as well, a hidden code, a specific body of knowledge relating to us. The awakening of the circles, that's the important thing here. Life will throw us together, it's a leap of faith, I know, but not one without a vision.'

Guisepe had it seemed the magic key to visions, and although he wasn't the only one in the group so blessed, he was in comparison a constant stream of them. As he closed his eyes to recall the images, everyone stirred and huddled together like little children ready to hear a good story, something exciting.

'It happened by the spring. I recall being confused that day, lost in the fabric woven by so many experiences, looking for the essence amidst the shadows cast by the density of my soul. I walked through the fog and lured by the soothing sound of the slowly flowing water I reached the dark pool by the spring and immersed my head in the cool liquid. As I lifted my head I saw the reflection of the moon drifting along the surface of the water, but it was a moonless night and when I looked at the sky I saw only stars; melodic light from countless trumpets carrying times past and future led me to the clearing. There, I saw my dead body bathed in the full moon's light and a procession of priestesses from some ancient time smudging it with incense as they chanted the words of a funeral rite. I saw a white thread as I descended in Hades to find the torch of resurrection that the Christ lit as he journeyed through – a light for the travellers of the mystical landscape. The black cloth of oblivion is tied around my eyes; I have to let go of everything for this trip. Darkness; I dream within the dream that I am in a village immersed in beautiful light, together with many friends gathered around a table laid bountifully with food. In front of me is a golden chalice containing a swirling black liquid. Darkness; I feel and I know that I am in a dark cave. Pitch dark on my right, but I could sense a dark pool of cold water there. Gradually, as my eyes opened further to embrace the dark I saw on the floor of the cave on my left a green dragon. It spat fire through its mouth illuminating its razor sharp teeth, yet it sat like a tame animal. I noticed a chain tied to his neck. Holding the chain with her left hand was a woman dressed in black, radiating a deep blue and green light. She stepped on the dragon's head and stars appeared on her head. Her smile had the joy that comes from the acceptance of immense pain and sorrow. 'The time has come,' she said pointing at the centre of the dark spiralling pool. 'Who are you beloved?' I asked, and she opened her hand; and I saw a star wrapping itself in earth and illuminating it from the inside. Like the moisture on the rock of the cave, I felt a tear running inside my heart. As I approached, I could barely see the water it was so black, only through the reflection of Her light on the surface could I tell where it was. I looked at Her again, and reassured as only She could, I jumped in the whirlpool head first. And I felt the water pull me down, deep in the Earth's guts, and through a narrow passage in the rock. High above me I could see a light through the water. I started to ascend slowly, almost as in slow motion edging up, effortlessly now, not gasping for breath. I felt the surface of the water as the top of my head touched it, then my eyes broke through and I kept rising, weightless, realising at the same time that I was made of light and not alone as I was walking now on the surface of this lake towards the shore. There were mountains all around, and as others were surfacing, I also saw tall luminous beings coming down through a mountain pass to the beach, Angels it turns out, come to meet us to lead us to the big table under the grape vine, where all the old friends were gathering for the Feast!'

The group's energy had lifted up with the vision, people happily floating in the feeling of future wellbeing!

'There is still a lot of work to be done on this end, let's not forget,' said Giusepe in a cautionary way. 'The journey is long, and by the looks of things we could well be busy in the meantime. There are smaller yet very significant cycles to go through.' In his heart he knew that the future for him was difficult, something very painful lying up ahead. Still, that was another lifetime, and there was still this one to deal with.

'It takes at least three to start things up, to locate the area in the higher consciousness where all this will be stored. And as it is that every leaf even on the same plant, is different and unique, so are we humans, and our vibrations are something like a signature in consciousness space. So the meeting of three of us – any three – will be enough to locate it. We are all 12 of us attuned to a higher place – a specific one, so that's the glue and focus. No doubt then, we need the whole group to come together, so that will follow.' Guisepe realised he was rambling, he'd lost their attention now, each withdrawn to their own thoughts, or carrying some conversation with a smaller group. 'They are like children,' he thought to himself, an uncomfortable thought entering his mind, as he remembered how in comparison to the rest of them he had a much more difficult time engendering lightness -his aura was usually heavy, or serious and intense but in any case not light and free like a child. This was one of his shortcomings he'd have to deal with eventually. And like so many times before he just set his feelings aside and focused on the next step, the job at hand, leaving all the sorting for 'another lifetime'.

The group had started dispersing into the night, goodbyes, see you then and the usual round of embraces, after all it was dangerous being a pagan mystic in this age and time and they all knew the risks. Guisepe waved his hand absentmindedly barely noticing what was going on, still immersed in his deep thinking.

Sometimes he thought that maybe he was mad, maybe all he experienced was an illusion created by his own mind, an overactive imagination gone astray. Sometimes he thought he was being devious, leading them on into their own death dangling the carrot of more to come later in front of their faces, sounding so convincing and yet it was all a big question mark in his own mind. Sometimes he wandered if it would really make any difference to anyone, ever, if they lived or died, if they had ever danced the spirit dance. Sometimes, just like many others, he doubted everything. But most of the time he himself at least was convinced that his experiences were real and meaningful, and that his visions did need to be acted out and acted upon.

'In any case,' he argued with himself in the now almost empty space, 'if it is my mind making it all up then it must really be quite a horrible reality out there, cold and empty, in which case we're probably better off fooling ourselves until we die.'

Tired from the eventful night, Guisepe took the short cut to his cottage in the woods. He sensed the presence inside as a friend before he even got to the door. None the less he took the precaution of drawing his dagger and holding it under his cloak before he swung the old door wide open. Halfway down the room, by the table, stood a tall man holding a book in his hand with his back turned. Guisepe recognised him instantly.

'John! You old pirate!' he shouted out stepping forward to embrace his good friend.

'Not so old yet you old wizard!' replied John as they hugged.

'Sit down, sit down,' beckoned Guisepe pulling the wooden chair out for him. 'How good to see you so unexpectedly, what brings you across and so far from home?' he asked as he paced about getting the fire going for some tea. John looked at him pensively, his left hand in his pocket scrunching a piece of paper, a note from Guisepe he'd received through Esme in Sicily – she had some business here with Guisepe not long ago, something she wouldn't discuss with him. The note had disturbed him, it seemed like the usual stuff, advice on all sorts of issues in a way, which made Guisepe something of a teacher to him, but it also had this sense of finality like they weren't going to be any more notes or meetings. In spite of the dangers of the trip, he was a wanted pirate after all, and the advice of his mates to wait for the next time he saw him, John had decided that if anything was about to happen he wanted to know and Guisepe was his friend, his good friend.

'It's this note,' he said finally, throwing it on the table. Guisepe picked it up and handed it back to John.

'Ah yes, the note I sent through Esmeralda, how is she anyway?' asked Guisepe warmly. He had the good fortune to work with the witch on a few occasions and had warmed up to her not only for her exceptional skills, but more for her imaginative use of the powers. John had come into the picture through her, when the island community was in trouble. They'd all pooled together their knowledge and guts and the result had been so far so good. A positive step towards a human utopia.

'She's fine, thank you. Now listen here Guisepe ... I don't mean to be inquisitive, I know there are things you don't tell me because if I get caught who knows, and anyway if I don't need to know that's fine with me. But ...' John paused to think how he should phrase his next thought, after all he didn't want Guisepe to think he came all this way- a journey of a few days- just because he was worried, even if he did. 'What I'm trying to say is ...'

'You're worried! That's what this is! You misread my note, and panicked!' cried out Guisepe almost hollering in laughter.

'No, not at all, I have some other business in Venice and I thought I must as well drop by ...' started John knowing that his friend wouldn't believe a word of what he just said.

'Come now, you know very well I can see right through you sometimes, and this is one of them! It's all right, my fault really, I did write the letter and I suppose it's better this way, it gives us an ... opportunity to talk again and I'd rather hand you the bundle myself ...' Guisepe stopped as he recalled the letter he'd written, he had wished that John would react to it but had to make sure anyway about the bundle. That was more important and shouldn't fall in the wrong hands.

'Well what do you expect, writing to me that you are hiding a bundle for me, and when I'm around here again I must pick it up and all that – and where are you going to be? And why leave such an important bundle instead of giving it to me the next time? Off for a long trip without saying goodbye? Yes, and before you say it I know – there are no goodbyes.' John had stood up now as Guisepe messed around with the cups and tea. He wandered further into the room. The walls were covered with shelves, full of unusual objects, glass bottles containing anything from herbal mixtures to bones, powdered roots, curious looking potions and books of course, piles of them. His eyes fell on a large animal skull. It sparked his curiosity and he held it up to look at it more closely.

'I see you found the bear skull. Be careful there, that's powerful magic,' offered Guisepe putting the cups on the table.

'Tell me about it,' said John. The skull had given him a jolt when he first touched it, and John felt there was something about it – he couldn't quite see it clearly – something like kinship, an inner growl.

'Remember that trip up the mountain in the North?' asked Guisepe.

'Yes, how could I forget! That was the one where all sorts of things happened, right from the start – quite an enchanted place that. The steep climb, the strange lights in the woods at night by our camp – spirits you said. And the eagles, those magnificent creatures, soaring ... yes I remember, what about it?'

'Well on that same mountain, high up there close to the summit before the last steepest climb that looks like a stone wall, there is a cave. It's a cave of bear magic, has been for hundreds of years. The shamans and later the druids would clothe themselves with bear skins and wear the bear skull on their head while dancing around the fire beating on drums and sacred rattles. The visions they would get would show them the ways of healing, using the plants of the earth and the power within them. Healing rituals would also be revealed to them. The bear magic circles have existed for a long time but now have gone in hiding like many others, including ourselves. This is one of the skulls from that cave, I've been ... working with it,' he said with a knowing smile in his face. 'But enough on the skull, you came here to find out something else,' he said still undecided as to how much of the plan he should tell his friend. Keeping secrets was awkward but sometimes necessary. 'Something big is going to happen, here in Venice and very soon,' he started saying staring right into John's eyes. 'Our circle here is deeply involved. As you know to some extent, we've been experimenting here with magic healing rituals for years. We've been open to anything that works, so long as it's for good of course, the criterion usually being that it results in healing knowledge. Lately, being moved by visions and "coincident occurrences" we've stumbled into something big. A space – on a higher plane – a space where possibilities are endless, a powerful place of a higher circle. In the process of working with this, things started to happen, subtle in the beginning, and then sometimes like a kick in the eye a sudden flash.'

'Alchemy, you stumbled into alchemy,' whispered John.

'Reminds me of that strange fellow, what was his name?' he asked.

'Solomon Trismosin, the sacred union. Yes and no,' replied Guisepe shaking his hands. 'Alchemy is our limited way of looking at a much bigger universe. For most it's the greed for material possession that drives them – gold. But for the few that seek the golden light of the Divine Spirit – no name does it justice but one has to express- alchemy is but a path onto the one path, beyond religion and belief. And what we found out was that by raising our vibration as a circle we actually became a sort of channel or bridge between this plane and that. We thought we discovered something new when in fact it is very old. From the first time people faced devastation they danced this dance, opened this space around the Sacred Fire. It is the acknowledgement of the nature of the Spirit and the sacredness of life that prepares the ground. It is the dancing that harmonises our pulsating soul with the pulse of nature. That opens the door to the spirit world. Many tribal religions have the memory of this dance embedded in their esoteric traditions somewhere. This is a dance that belongs to no religion because it exists on the one path, the true path beyond religion and race. It belongs to all of humanity, it's the dance of the one people come together, it belongs to all of us, those before us and those yet to come.

'I won't bore you with the details, but essentially what we plan to do is to bust open the gates between the two worlds right under their noses at the Dodge's wedding.' John's jaw dropped momentarily.

'Did I hear that right?' he exclaimed with incredulity.

'You plan to go to the big wedding, where all the soldiers will be – they are hunting down witches by the way just in case you forgot even here in Venice, so you'll be doing some pagan type ritual, and ... why? Why on that day of all days, and why there? Have you lost your mind? Are you on some sort of death wish?'

'Not at all, life is precious and to be cherished. As to the why then, well it has to do with the stars, the signs are right and the time is set. As to the place, it just happens to be the precise kind of power spot we need for this. This is precisely why they built the cathedral in that spot, which of course happens a lot. Any new religion, no matter what story it uses to mould its followers can't ignore the obvious sources of energy on the planet, and to have power they must control them. This is where we come in, starting a chain reaction by breaking that balance and grounding heavenly energy to heal the Earth itself from the evils of our world. Trismosin was onto something, the sacred union of light and darkness does exist and is available to us humans. It's just not how he imagined it, nor in that direction. What it is in reality is an alchemical transmutation of the body and soul by the spirit. This is not a vision I'm describing, it's a tangible effect. When we dance the circle dance of the sacred union our bodies change. It's not a permanent state, not yet, but the experience of light is different, and for a short while the body itself gives off a visible light. But nothing is without sacrifice.' Guisepe got up and moved around the room. He feared he'd probably said too much already and wondered if John had listened. 'So that's that,' he concluded somewhat unceremoniously.

'Now hold on, you can't do that, just like the damn letter!' John protested. He was more down to earth than this Venetian lot but knew enough about magic and mysticism to read the danger signs. 'Well at least we're past the animal sacrifices!' he said trying to get a reaction by make light of the matter.

'Nothing is achieved without sacrifice. The ultimate prize requires the ultimate sacrifice,' came the reply from the other end of the room.

'Now you're scaring me ... surely you refer to the sacrifice of the self to be of service to others ...' John's voice sounded more like a boy's now rather than the hardened pirate he really was. Guisepe noted that in his mind.

'Maybe Esmeralda has had more of an influence than I thought,' he replied, trying to lighten the conversation. John shrugged his shoulders sheepishly. 'What is sacred must be observed and not ignored. If we who have seen something more with our eyes than most didn't act upon what has been revealed to us, who will? And what would the point of living be if we couldn't do something to end this farce, to jolt this complacent world out of its spiritual slumber? To stop this endless warring and killing, all the suffering and pain.' Guisepe moved around as if he was looking for something. He stuck his hand in the wall through some concealed opening covered by books and brought out a leather bundle.

'Aha, found it!' he declared. He was eager to end the conversation and focus John's mind on something else. This could be just the thing he thought as he gently laid the bundle on the table. He started unwrapping the animal skin. 'This bundle came recently from the New World.

Perceptions vary on this, but if you ask the right people, someone who can see a thing or two still, you get the impression that the natives there are people of the Earth, they worship One God, and they live lives very close to what the Creator intended all of us to live. Simple lives but close to the Earth, still in touch with the early mysteries and ways of power. This here is a medicine bundle, a healing tool. Inside the four layers of animal hide – some kind of wild four legged creature resembling a big bull but hairy- is this . . .' Guisepe lifted the last layer to reveal a red stone pipe and next to it a long wooden stem. By the stem was a bunch of feathers from a large bird, each tied up in different colour thread. 'It's a healing pipe used in a number of ceremonies of Earth and Sky magic. I'm not sure how it works, but the person who gave it to me said that you must keep the stem separate from the stone bowl and connect them only during the ritual because that's what activates it. He also said that if you pray for guidance, the pipe itself will reveal how it wants to be handled.'

'Is it all right if I touch it?' asked John eagerly.

'Just as I expected you already know that it's sacred and you have the right attitude towards it. Yes, you should touch it, it is for you to carry now and more importantly to use,' replied Guisepe whilst motioning with his hands for John to go ahead. He didn't need further encouragement. He lifted the stem and the red stone pipe and bringing them to his chest connected them.

'Are you sure this is activated now?' he asked with incredulity.

'You are supposed to smoke through it, the natives use

some tree bark but I suspect any smoking herb will do. I prepared a mixture for you to take with you because I want you to be able to use it as soon as you need it, it's mostly mullein, with some bear berry leaf, and skullcap.' Guisepe unhooked a small leather pouch from a hook on one of the slanted roof's rafters and placed it on the table next to the hides. John was still holding the pipe in the air.

'So what's with the carvings?' he asked turning the wooden shaft towards Guisepe. On the top of it were carvings of three animals.

'The turtle apparently symbolises the New World where they have lived for thousands of years. The next one is that animal who's hide they used to wrap it up, I don't know its name but it's very sacred to them – they use it for food but also its hides for their homes and clothes. The last one is a bear. The feathers are eagle feathers, so there you have the sky element. The pipe, including the people who smoke it in ritual, represents all that is, and it underlines the Oneness of creation. That alone to me is enough to make this a sacred object, but I sense that there is a period of acquaintance, a period of prayer before you'll be able to use it properly. It's like learning a new skill, just takes time and the right attitude.'

'Why me then Guisepe? I have neither time, with all the work that goes into keeping the community going, nor do I have the attitude for it. This is much more Esme's field, healing and such, and yours. Either of you would definitely be more qualified to handle this and use it right. Me, I'm more of a warrior as you well know.' John was getting that feeling again, the same one that spurred him to Venice in the first place. 'Your trying to dance around this one I can see, but why?' It was more than a question, it was a demand to know. In his own mind John was contemplating the many negative thoughts that seemed to be welling up. 'And why did you say I'll be needing this soon? I didn't know that fortune telling was one of your skills – new one?' Guisepe knew that it wasn't going to end until John was satisfied that all would be well. Had he thought of this eventuality earlier he could have slipped something in his tea to drug him but it was too late for that now. He had to do something.

'Things change,' he started, 'and you might grow to find that healing is the only way for you, it will give you what you need. We all have our path to walk and nobody else can do that for us.' Guisepe was pacing up and down, moving around the room biding his time while he got in the right position. Using all his skill as a stalker and his knowledge as a healer wasn't enough. He needed something heavy, but not sharp. All in one move he grabbed a bottle of rum from the shelf and smashed it over the unsuspecting John's head. Guisepe caught him before he fell to the floor and cushioned the impact. He examined the cut and swiftly made up some poultice for it to heal fast. As he picked the little pieces of glass from his hair he held his friend on his lap and gently whispered: 'Farewell my friend. I pray I'm right and we'll meet again, some other life time, some other place. If I'm wrong then forgive me for I still have to go with what my heart tells me . . . I love you.' He moved fast and using the rug he dragged him along the floor and past the door. Once outside he struggled to get him on his back but once he managed to balance him there he moved through the woods at a good pace. The night had finished its journey and was pulling its cloak back drawing the light of the new dawn over the distant horizon.

☯

'It's all happening at once,' he thought reflecting on the almost continuous stream of events that took place in one night. 'That's a good sign, means we are getting close to a real event.' Soon he reached some trusted friends' home and strapped John onto a horse. 'Take him west, all the way to the shore. Go past Ferrara and Modena, but stay clear of Bologna, the knights around there are all over the countryside there, there's been some trouble recently. Try to get to Luca, I've got some friends there, look for Victor Pisante at the Drunken Mare, a tavern on the south side. A man of real heart and extremely intelligent, you can trust him with your life. He's a Jew, fleeing from Spain like many others, moved to Pisa a couple of years ago. He'll help you get a boat down the Arno river. Where that reaches the sea John will be able to hook up with a larger boat to take him over to his ship. When he comes to give him this to drink for his head and tell him that Guisepe said he must make his way back to the community immediately because I have gotten word that they need him urgently. Tell him there is no time to lose; lives depend on it – that will keep him from trying to come back here first. Be careful not to arouse any suspicion at any check points, he is wanted and someone might recognise him. I'll see you in a couple of days when you return. May the spirit be with you – go now!'

'And with you my friend!' replied Alexandro as he dug

his heels into his horse's side. The trail was uphill and he had the other horse in tow but the powerful animal was spirited and soon the two horses had vanished through the thick forest.

The long trail started unfolding as the horses hooves hit the rocky ground. Alexandro contemplated the potential dangers that they were more than likely going to encounter on route. They'd still be in Venetian territory until the afternoon, but after that . . . this part of the world was full of Republics and Duchys and on this short journey alone they would have to cross at least five territorial borders. Camped in the vicinity of the main roads connecting the big towns you could find a diverse selection of ruthless villains, some wearing the knight's armour some not. Most were in the employ of the local state, and when there was no war to fight in, and foreign territories to pillage – a rarity these days – they tended to supplement their income by stealing from any travellers who didn't have the right connections and papers, and who were thankful to be spared their lives. Oh it's so easy to be branded an enemy of the state, especially with so many states to choose from! And as if the home grown ones weren't enough, there was always Spain, France and the English. Louis XII's French army had just recently taken over the Duchy of Milan. The Spanish, Ferdinand of Aragon and Isabella of Castille, controlled Sardinia and Sicily. And speaking of enemies of the state, he was travelling with one wanted by all of them. No one liked a rebel, especially one they couldn't control.

Alexandro had already decided to take the rougher trails, suitable only for horses and mules but too narrow for anything with wheels on it, potentially carrying a valuable load. 'Fewer soldiers and thieves, so less hassle,' he thought. Eventually he'd have to deal with John, but in the meantime he had to stay out everyone's sight; carrying another man bound to his horse was certain to invite unwanted attention. He stuck to the thick woods as much as he could, and when he had to cross open ground he balanced caution with speed.

Something that Guisepe had said came to his mind. It had seemed odd at the time, but then again these were exceptional circumstances and he hadn't had the time to think about it anyway. But it seemed odd that Guisepe had said 'see you in a couple of days when you return', Guisepe knew well the journey would take closer to a week altogether. It wasn't anything major, except that Guisepe prided himself on his verbal accuracy, and was always a man with a plan, someone whom you could count on to be definite and detailed about the happenings in the next four weeks, let alone a few days. 'No, he was definitely being very vague, as if he wasn't at all sure what was going to happen next,' thought Alexandro. '... and in any case, by the time I'm back it will have happened and he can tell me all about it.'

After a while he spotted a good resting place for the horses, next to a small stream on the edge of the woods with a good view of the surroundings. Alexandro decided it was safe enough to rest and have some of the food his wife packed for them. John was starting to wriggle about after he lay him on the grassy verge. He loosened his ropes just enough so he could untie himself, stuck his dagger in the ground in front of him and moved back a couple of paces.

'As you can see I'm a friend, so don't cut me up, just ask me and I'll answer,' he said as he sipped some water from his flask.

'Ask you what?' came the voice from the pirate, his eyes fixed on the dagger, his hands nimbly untying the ropes. As soon as he had managed to free his hands he grabbed the dagger and cut the ropes from his feet in one move, ending up standing and pointing the blade to Alexandro's throat. He calmly extended his arm offering John the flask.

'Here, you must be thirsty. And give me back my dagger when you're done playing with it, yours is in the saddle bag,' he said. John hesitated for a second, his mind piecing together the last memories of being in Guisepe's cabin in the woods. He took the flask but kept the dagger in his hand by his side. 'Guisepe brought you over to me with instructions to take you across land to the western coast. He specifically said to tell you that you must get back to the island urgently, some sort of serious trouble and you mustn't waste time. Oh, and he gave me this,' he said pulling out a small glass bottle from his bag, 'for the headache, as I understand he bashed you a good one. Now Guisepe is a good friend of mine, and for him to do that to you he must have a good reason – but all in your own time, I realise you must be confused.' Alesandro sat down, and unwrapped a cloth with a loaf of bread, some hard cheese, tomatoes and olives in it. 'My dagger, if you don't mind,' he said extending his arm. John turned it over in his hand and passed him the blade, handle first. Alexandro motioned for him to sit down. 'We've got a long way to go, but the horses need to rest, we've been riding since dawn,' he said pointing to the Sun low in the sky. John sat next to him and had some food. He was unsettled about Guisepe's plans before he saw him, and even more so now that he had smashed a bottle on his head. But the message about the island community was alarming. He had to go back now, he had no choice. There was no point in going back to Venice; Guisepe hadn't wanted him around obviously, and wasn't going to make himself available for questioning, even if John had been able to find him, and that alone could take days.

'Well, let's not waste any time, the horses look rested enough and we need to use the daylight,' he said getting up and walking towards his horse. 'But tell me, what do you make of all this?' he added as he started saddling up.

'I don't know, but I've got a bad feeling about it. Guisepe is acting very strangely, even for his standards. I know he and his circle are planning something big, and it seems it will be soon. There's also the big wedding coming up and the secret police have been working overtime rounding up the likely troublemakers. But most of all it's the bloody inquisition that frightens me. I mean we're relatively safe in Venice, but the corrupt church is always a concern, and in the south the witch burnings go on. Real evil bastards them Christians!' John nodded. He knew what Alexandro was talking about. Many of the children in his island utopia were orphans, whose parents had rightly or wrongly been identified as witches and burnt at the stake. He'd taken a special interest in them, being once such a child himself. He always sought to recover them whenever he'd gotten news of any drifting about.

Thankfully the community always regarded children as a blessing, as life was difficult and many little ones never made it through early childhood. His thoughts spurred him on, and soon they were galloping along the edge of the forest.

Guisepe was strolling around Venice's Plaza di San Marco. The day had been declared a holiday because of the wedding, and the usual groups of tradesmen and workers had gathered to fight for the possession of yet another wooden bridge in the city. Guisepe had always wondered about what drove grown men to spend their Sunday afternoons beating each other with big long sticks in order to hold a bridge for a few hours. 'Then again,' he thought 'I wonder what they would make of us, dancing around a fire all night for a vision!' He walked around aimlessly, blending with the crowd whilst making mental notes of the secret police and their positions in the square. 'This will remove any doubts from their minds if they still have any about our plans,' he thought and made a long stop by the old side entrance to the cathedral's basement. He was well aware that he was being followed, ever since the market. He was known to them, but they wouldn't arrest him now, not before the whole group arrived, so he felt safe enough to perform the act of surveying the setting before the crime – after all it was expected. He'd have to shake him soon, now was a good opportunity, going over the bridge. A group of five men dressed with identical clothes to him was waiting on top. He stepped amongst them and moments later the group broke up and dispersed in every possible direction like a fan. The secret policeman that was tailing him jumped up and down and then motioned his arms. Out of nowhere there was movement and soon all five had a tail on them. Guisepe looked on, surprised by their efficiency. 'They're more prepared than I thought,' he murmured.

'Yes, well let's get off this bridge before they figure out what happened,' suggested Franco. 'And you better find somewhere to change back into your own clothes, or you might get arrested for vagrancy!' he chuckled trying to control himself. On the top of the new Clock Tower the two bronze Moors beat their heavy hammers on the huge bell to mark midday. Underneath, on the outside of the clock's face another dial pointed to the half waxing moon. It was a time of transition, a door waiting to be opened.

A few minutes later they were sitting comfortably in the dark corner of a local tavern. 'Change of plans,' announced Guisepe. Franco leaned over.

'What do you mean change of plans? Is something wrong?' he asked, his wrinkled forehead underlining the tension in his voice.

'No, nothing's wrong, it's all according to plan. Only the plan is a bit different than what I've told you. I took the precaution of baiting them and pulling them into our fold. They would try and find out anyway so I decided to play it safe and give them the plan, the one I gave you all whilst keeping the real details in my mind only.'

'You devious fox!' remarked Franco. 'You bastard as well for not trusting us!'

'Oh, I trust you all of course, have no doubt. But I

also had trust that they would have ears close to us, and I was right as you can see from today alone! Whoever it is they are very close, so you are going to have to get in touch with the rest personally, and make absolutely sure nobody overhears you when you give out the new meeting place, agreed?' asked Guisepe holding firmly onto Franco's arm.

'Yes, of course. So where is it going to be?' he replied.

'At the old garden site, where the ancient ruins are. We've been there together, remember? Years ago.' Franco nodded.

'Well that sounds much better than the basement. I was never that convinced that one would have worked.' Franco sat back and gulped the rest of his wine down his throat. 'I better go find them then, I've got a good idea where . . . Be safe. Still sunset I presume?'

'Yes, see you there,' said Guisepe. They walked out separately. When he walked out of the smoky room into the alley Guisepe could see no sign of Franco. He was confident that he would find the others in time by himself, so he'd decided to do the rounds, visiting the people he cared most for and some of his enemies. There was more to arrange before nightfall.

☯

At the garden, by the old ruins of the temple of Artemis, an odd group had assembled in the long shadows of the tall cypress trees. The Sun was setting through the low thin and outstretched clouds, bursting through them in deep fiery colours. 'Why is he not here yet?' asked Thomaso.

'Ssh! I can hear someone coming!' whispered Franco. Guisepe appeared from behind a big boulder.

'Finally, you're here!' exclaimed Thomaso.

'We said sunset. Anyway I had a few things to do . . . are we all here?' asked Guisepe looking around at the group.

'All here,' replied Franco, 'and ready,' he added.

'Well let's begin then,' he announced. The group moved out to where the circular marble floor of the old temple was and started preparing the ground. The garden was in fact quite a large area, overgrown with all sorts of plants, some patches of silver birch, and oak, and quite a lot of pine and cypress trees. Although close to the town it also provided some privacy, and in the day one could often stumble upon some young lovers looking for a quiet corner to share their bodies with each other. At night though nobody went close to the place, it was too overgrown and the temple ruins often visited by unruly pagans.

Guisepe went around the circle and embraced each one there. 'I am ready now,' he declared. They all joined hands and began chanting.

'AAAAAAAUUUUUUUMMMMMMMMMMM'

Shimmering silver light moved around the circle gathering speed. Guisepe raised his eyes to the night sky and whilst the chanting continued he said:

'Divine Creator, to You who has made everything that is, who clothed us with this Earth so we can be part of Her, who is the fire within our souls, Sacred Spirit who moves in all things, listen to our prayers. Great evil is taking over our world, and your people, the people of this earth are suffering. You have given us the medicine for our bodies in the plants of this Earth, and the sacred ways to prepare and use them for the healing of the body and the soul, but in so doing they call us witches and wizards and burn us at the stake. Listen to the cries of the tortured, the tears of the martyrs for they are many . . . .' The chanting was by now a barely audible humming sound. 'We raise our arms together in this sacred circle, to show we are One with all life on this Earth, reaching up to the Sky, a bridge for your Mercy. Our dance around the sacred fire is our prayer. As we feel the Earth with our feet and raise our hands towards the Sky we pray for all the Sacred Circles that were here before us to join us in this sacred dance, to help us awaken this world of pain to the light of Your Healing Love.'

They lowered their hands and let go of each other without breaking the circle. By the fire on a spread out blanket were some rattles, drums, bells and whistles. The drum skins had been heated by the fire and were ready to beat on. One by one they visited the blanket and picked up a sound maker. Then, each with a different animal cry they would run around the fire and spiral into the dancing circle. By the fire the drummers were trancing on an ever changing beat. The dancing got wilder and wilder and the drumming deep and furious. In the calm of the night a strong wind seemed to rise, but it was only around the circle itself. It felt to Franco like being in a whirlwind, one that wasn't travelling anywhere. Guisepe was like the rest of them dancing wildly around the fire to a beat he'd never heard before, uttering cries he couldn't recognise, some human, some animal.

He barely noticed it at first, a change in the intensity and the quality of the light. It was more of an orange colour turning golden with white swirls here and there. But then the swirls unfolded into figures, made of white light like ghosts. Some of them looked much like themselves, but some looked like they were from a time long past. They wore animal hides with feathers and bones on them. Guisepe recognised the wolf, bear, lion, panther and crocodile. He realised, as they all did, that not only the martyrs of this age but also the shamans of past times had joined them in their sacred dance. Guisepe felt the heavy oak doors of his inner heart being blown open by the golden light. Tears of joy were streaming from his eyes, and felt like liquid fire on his face.

Looking around the circle as he kept on dancing he could barely recognise his friends, they all seemed to be glowing bright. All his life he worked for this moment, not waiting, but searching and experimenting, asking and receiving. To open this sacred space with his friends, to bring it that much closer to its manifestation on this Earth, to bring an end to all the needless suffering. He'd had his doubts of course, who wouldn't? Was it even possible, had it been tried before, would it work? Well now he knew for sure it wasn't the first time, as he suspected from the start when the possibility however remote first occurred to him. It had been a gift, he realised this now, not a reward but a confirmation of his good work. To dance the dance of humanity's salvation in such holy company! 'Thank You!' he howled. Just behind him on his right the spirit dancer of a shaman wearing a bear skull and hide was dancing a foot above the ground. He extended his left arm and touched Guisepe on his shoulder who instantly recognised him as one of his spirit guides. The shaman smiled at him, then came along his side and pointed with his eyes. Guisepe smiled back and turned to his left. He'd almost forgotten about his companion, his ever present friend. The velvety black cloak he could always see if he wanted to, but now for the first time he could see inside the hood's eternal dark void, a human skull, his own skull. 'I'm ready,' he whispered.

The arrows flew in from all directions with the force and accuracy of a crossbow fired at close range. The dancers dropped to the ground like wounded animals taken by surprise and still moving. The arrows suddenly stopped whizzing. The sound of many blades being drawn, for the kill. Guisepe and Franco were the only ones left unscathed, their ten friends lying on the ground, wounded or dead already. They looked at each other and smiled drawing their blades.

'I want those two alive!' came a commanding voice through the darkness. The two friends charged pointing their blade at each others' heart. It was done. Nothing could stop them now.

'You idiots! I told you to stop them, I wanted some information ... oh well, bunch of useless morons ...' The commander of the small force was soon joined by one of the city's patriarchs sent by the council to keep the dog on a short leash.

'What's all this?' he asked in an authoritative tone.

'Oh, just some cleaning up ...' replied the unwilling commander, who detested the controls of the politicians in his work. It was all right for them to pontificate on all the virtues of the city, entertaining themselves steeped in luxury in the vast palaces inspired by their amazing murals, but what did he get? Nothing but the dirty work, a pat in the back and some meagre increase in wages. Whilst the man from Aragon paid gold coins for every witch.

'Looks more like a blood bath to me. Who are all these admittedly pagan dressed folks and why have you resorted to this?' the patriarch's tone of voice was threatening, reminding the commander of his impatience with subordinates.

'A circle of witches and wizards my Lord, Satan worshipers as you yourself can see. Just look at the animal skulls, and all this primitive paraphernalia they carry on their bodies. I tried to arrest the leaders but they killed each other – no stomach for torture I expect, not like a real man.' The commander straightened his back and puffed his chest out a bit more.

'Since when are we hunting down witches here in Venice commander? Our policies are strictly neutral to this inquisition business, as you well know. Speak up man, I've got no time to waste with you!' he shouted in reply.

'Not just any circle this one my Lord. Dangerous subversives, plotting against the council no doubt,' replied the commander. 'We've been keeping an eye on them for months now, and today we received information that they were going to carry out something big in this garden so we intercepted them.'

'Looks more like a massacre to me. Apart from those two embraced bodies down there the rest aren't even holding a weapon! Unless you count the rattle there, I can see how that can be dangerous, and those drums are quite big and heavy . . . do you take me for a fool?!' shouted the patriarch.

'No my Lord,' responded the commander apologetically and yet refusing to offer any other explanation.

'Just bury them, and keep it all quiet. We don't want any distractions from the celebrations, there are a lot of important people in the city tonight and I don't want them disturbed by any of this, understood?' The patriarch suspected the involvement of the inquisition in this, it would be easy to bribe an officer and he didn't trust this commander, a ruthless man of little intellect. Never the less there was no need to make enemies of him, or any high ranking secret policeman and risk his own body to be found floating down the canals one of these days.

'Yes my Lord,' came the cold reply.

When the politician had left, the commander ordered his men to dig a big pit on site. 'We might as well bury them here than drag them about. The council has already decided to make the new city cemetery over this cursed pagan ruins anyway to stop them from using it, so we'll inaugurate it ourselves. And throw all those animal skulls and stuff in there as well.'

The night was dark, the moon had already set and dawn was still some time away. In the garden, an owl's persistent hooting rose above the scraping sound of the soldier's spades cutting the blood soaked ground. A pair of tearful eyes disappeared behind the trees.

CHAPTER 5
ABOUT DEATH

Nigh time in the big city. For some a time for fun, for others a dangerous time.

The interstate highway bridge by the homeless shelter provided a close by dry spot, just right for a drink in the rain.

'Here, have some of this,' said Frank, passing the bottle of pure white 'Thunderbird' alcohol, which tasted something between Gin and Vodka if that's at all possible. The smell was so potent that instinctively Andri moved his cigarette well clear of the bottle.

'Hmm, thanks,' he said passing it back to Frank who was certainly ready to gulp another big swig. The rumbling of the bridge under the weight of the fast moving night time traffic softened the sharp sound of the ambulance sirens approaching the city hospital, just down the road. The bridge, an old structure made of metal, which would soon need some attention, was a host to a lot of traffic underneath as well, cardboard boxes lined up on the side with an assortment of plastic sheeting and bags through which you could barely discern someone's hat and face. Frank, who once used to be a banker, before his wife left him, and he started drinking too much, then 'it was all downhill from there,' as he'd told Andri once. Andri had been working at the Pine Street Inn shelter for the homeless for a year now, and had gotten to know a few of the regulars quite well. Although treating someone for scabies or fleas was often a barrier breaking experience, many of the homeless just kept to themselves. The 'generous' social state had recently pulled the plug on funding for mental hospitals and half-way houses, who in turn had little choice but to discharge a lot of their mental patients, resulting in a big increase in homeless people in the city. The officials must have been so surprised when they found out that people suffering from severe mental problems cannot take care of themselves, like get a job, a place to live and all that basic stuff. If there ever was a safety net it certainly had some big holes.

'Ahh, this is good,' said Frank, taking another big gulp and almost falling backwards. Andri had noticed how pale Frank looked lately, he seemed to be drinking even more now than when he first met him at the Inn. People seemed to want to talk to him, not many, but those that did would go on and on about their life, their mistakes, missed opportunities, injustice. It was always a good confession, and often very emotional, and Andri had come to accept it, not being taken aback any more when it happened. The Inn itself was a little island of relative safety in a very badass urban jungle. You could easily get stabbed just outside for some cigarettes or booze, and as easily you could get shot at just a couple of streets away, as the Inn was on the edge

Boston, and the Archbishop. The State had provided the rest of the funding for decorations and small gifts, one per person 'as long as stocks last' was the big joke. 'Don't worry, they'll be enough for everyone,' the manager had insisted reassuringly when faced by accusations from some old timers. They wouldn't be a problem of course, the homeless who would be allowed in the room during the presence of the TV cameras had already been vetted, the most pleasant and least vocal ones as a general criterion. Why on earth they had to make all these sandwiches when there would be plenty of turkey coming? 'Well some people don't like turkey,' they had been informed. They would much prefer a ham sandwich or peanut butter and jelly. This had seemed a bit suspect to Andri, who apparently had been listening to 'the wrong crowd, them troublemakers, ungrateful lot!' Time was running out for complaints though, the TV crew had been set up in the morning, then dismantled (too much of a safety risk to the equipment) and set up once again. The back door bell rang. The caterers had brought the much talked about Christmas meal, all ready to be served in nice coloured plates with all the trimmings, it looked great, but enough for maybe 500 people at most.

Suddenly it was show time. The politicians and church leaders arrived in their limos, police escort of course amidst great noise and Christmas carols blaring on the loudspeakers. As the cameras rolled on, the crowd of dignitaries followed to the big hall, somewhat uneasy at the starkness of the atmosphere, for in spite of the valiant efforts of some of the staff and the homeless to decorate the hall in bright colours, the institutional green and grey still showed, and there was no way to disguise the rough looks on the faces of the gathered homeless. A couple of 'touching' Christmas speeches later, and after the Governor and Archbishop had both had the opportunity to be taken by the camera serving someone some food, or giving a gift to the 'grateful' homeless, they were gone. The turkey and gifts had ran out, the TV crew had wrapped everything up real polite and quick like and were gone, and the food was back to sandwiches. The whole thing must have taken at most half an hour, and by the rush of the dignitaries to get out of there you could tell they had somewhere real important to go to. A show, for the TV, public appeasement to keep Christmas 'a feel good time' so they can keep on spending more than they can afford, and eat more than they should.

☯

Andri was still wrapped up in his thoughts when he reached the subway station. He liked walking, and had rarely felt threatened even when walking in rough areas so he'd often walk through town all the way back home but the night had taken its toll so he took the steps down to the platform. The morning light was now pushing the shadows of the night away, and even under the ground it had found its way through the stairway to the cold metal rails. Just on the edge a man, passed out, one arm hanging in the void over the electrified wires. Andri approached him cautiously, and after a quick assessment went up to find a rail guard. As it happened he didn't have to look far, and soon a police car had arrived to take him away.

'Another one for the Inn,' the cop had said in a surprisingly empathetic voice.

On the train he couldn't shake the encounter with Frank earlier in the night. The thought of a man so alone in the world that approaching death – he was obviously ill and probably wouldn't last long – he had but one person to remember him, a counsellor in a homeless shelter. Granted, he wasn't a stranger to him anymore, they'd soon overcome the role thing and met as humans beings, friends. Yet the carer and client relationship was always there, there was a boundary – there had to be. Andri had seen again and again how dangerous it was to cross that boundary and how it had resulted in some cases he knew where the councillor ended up being homeless himself. He'd seen the burn out as well, and knew that he had to keep some distance if he wanted to keep at it for longer.

He picked up a bright yellow flyer from the dirty carriage floor and read it.

> *"People in Boston are dying for housing ... 14 last summer. The streets are nowhere to live, yet 12,500 people in Boston this year are doing just that. Sometimes they can't ..."* It was a call for a memorial service and march to put pressure on the state governor who refused to fund the Affordable Housing Act.

Death was on his mind, but that was nothing new. He often thought of death, often felt death next to him, following him a step behind, just inside the blind spot where you can't entirely see him. But death was to him like an old friend, familiar and comforting, and although he couldn't quite place since when he felt that way he knew it was from his childhood years. As far as he was concerned his own death was not something that frightened him but more of a security blanket, something to experience at a later date, after all the work had been done hopefully. When others close to him died he always had mixed feelings. Part of him was torn up from the slow realisation that he wouldn't see that person again, that the body is back in the ground, reclaimed by the Earth and assimilated into new life forms. Yet he also felt a certainty that something of the uniqueness of the person goes on, that which really touched you, not an image any more but the real thing. A bundle of light. And when he cried, alone at night, he knew that he cried for himself, his own loneliness missing the friend that left. At funerals he never cried, and almost felt insensitive to have such a casual approach to dying but couldn't help feeling this way.

His mother had often tried to shield him from the experience, by not telling him for example of his grandfather's on his father's side of the family funeral until after it happened. She must have forgotten how when he was little in elementary school, one of his classmates died from leukaemia, and everyone knew he was going to die for at least a year before it happened. They all marvelled as they watched their friend go through it, always a smile in his face and the joy of another day lived rather than the pain of regular blood transfusions and the fear of loss of all he knows. This lad was so brave that he tried to come to school 'till the very end, and he did, in spite of the pain, to savour every last experience in this life that he could.

'He taught us all how precious life really is,' he though. In the background he could hear the monotonous clatter of the subway train as the wheels went over the little gaps between each rail. The gaps were more pronounced in the sharp bend leading to the bridge over the Charles river, and Andri automatically raised his head to look outside as they crossed. The river was well frozen by now, the ice thick enough to drive a truck on it, and it wouldn't melt entirely 'till the end of March. On a cold winter day there were few sights as pretty as the area around the river, grassy banks now covered by a blanket of snow, sleeping trees covered by a layer of ice, icicles hanging from the branches like Christmas decorations. At the end of the bridge the train plunged underground again, the clattering interrupted by the loudspeaker announcing the next stop. 'MIT next stop, MIT. Please watch your step as you disembark.'

'Another couple of stops and I can get out in the light,' he thought relishing the crisp clean morning air.

Although he felt Death's presence always close to him, he could never see his face – nor did he think he ought to really- but he could see his black robe, something like shining velvet, the deepest 'outer space where there is no light for millions of years' kind of black, the kind of black that is so dense that it draws the light in. And he'd seen him up close in undesirable circumstances more than once. In fact it was at least three times in his lifetime that he'd barely escaped death, and each time he'd have this feeling, like it wasn't his time yet and someone had protected him. The story of his grandfather came to his mind. It was just after the second world war, and his father's family had moved to Athens to run a small grocery shop. The civil war between the communists and the fascists was still going on, and often enough in the mêlée someone would find opportunity to settle old grudges, whether stemming from political differences or not being besides the point. Andri's grandfather was sitting on a wooden rocking chair by the back door overlooking a small garden. He was reading a newspaper and rocking back and forth rhythmically in the soft early evening light when for no apparent reason he stopped. At the same moment somebody squeezed the trigger and a riffle shot pierced the air, burying a bullet on the wooden casing of the door right behind where his grandfather's head would be if he hadn't so suddenly stopped rocking. Later he'd found the empty shell behind the bushes. Maybe it was his wife calling him, or something he read in the news, a coincidence, but Andri believed that coincidence is the just one face of something unseen, a guardian force. The shell was still in display somewhere on his father's bookcase, a reminder of where it could have ended.

'Porter square next stop, Porter square!' The tinny sound from the speaker focused him on the time to get up and ready mode. Soon, he was walking up the stairs and through the glass cage out to the freezing winter air, the hard dirty snow by the roadside adding to the bleakness of Porter square, mostly a big car park with surrounding stores, supermarket, small diners and cafes, banks and laundry. He trudged along the avenue on the icy sidewalk, kicking the snow with his heavy leather boots and was soon heading up the hill to the warmth of home.

☯

He shut the door, threw his heavy coat on the bed in his room and then parked his body on the couch in the living room. He lit a cigarette and had a couple of drags letting the smoke slowly escape from his nostrils.

Images of death kept knocking on the door of his mind. He recalled Helen's funeral, the mother of a childhood friend who had recently jumped out of a balcony. Why did people give up? What on Earth could steal away any hope of things improving in someone's life? He'd gone to the church funeral and the burial, but hadn't had the chance to say goodbye, he needed more space so he'd gone back to the grave when everyone else had left. Two shovels were standing there, stuck in the mound of soil next to the grave waiting for the gravediggers to come back and finish the job. The sky was clear, had been all day, but out of nowhere it seemed it had started to drizzle. He'd stood there taking it all in. The brief rain had cleared the air from the city's smog and all the flowery smells of early Spring had been released. He felt she was still there, he could feel her essence hovering above the half buried coffin, a sweet presence – a faint light.

'I'm sorry you left so early. I love you. Have a good journey.' He'd felt that she had smiled at him and tears had come streaming out.

Andri had recalled that experience, and like on other occasions he hadn't said anything to anyone, out of fear they would only ridicule him. Anyway, most people avoided talking about death too seriously. 'It's those social constraints,' he thought, 'we're all so tied up with the do's and don'ts that whatever the truth is we're most likely to miss it anyway.' But what was the truth of the matter after all? How sure could he be that there was something like a spirit and soul which goes on living when the physical body dies? Is it not just a romantic notion, that we will see our departed friends again, not being able to face up to the alternative, that we don't. And if we don't, if 'all we are is dust in the wind' as the Kansas song goes, then how much more important to do what's right, to reach our potential as human beings, to be of service to others. Sure, we could take the attitude, like some, that we don't give a fuck, and if it's all limited to the physical then why not just enjoy as much as we can, let's be hedonists before it's all over! But still, how can we live like that when others suffer so, and not react in some way? How can we live like that when *we* suffer, as we do because we're so out of balance with nature, we've lost touch with the living planet we live on, including the plants and animals. We're unfulfilled – distanced from living within the sacred hoop of life as our Native American brothers say. It's all wrong, and can we change it? Are we really alone in a world of chance?

'You look like you're on another planet,' mused Vincent who had just come in using the back staircase. '... You all right?' he added, sensing perhaps the heaviness in the air.

'Yes, fine thanks my friend. Just milling over my mind some of those difficult questions, you know, is there really life after death or are we just fooling ourselves because it suits us? And therefore is there a God, a spiritual world, or is that just another deception fed to us by the Church?' replied Andri, re-adjusting his body on the couch to face Vincent and to reach over to the loaded pipe that seemed to appear in his hand out of nowhere. Vincent had been studying theology, although he talked more about politics than anything else, but it was obviously a question he'd pondered in some depth.

'I think it's a dangerous thing this life after death belief,' he started to say only to be interrupted by the arrival of Nash, another roommate who was also a theology student, the one actually who had discovered the house for the group to move into. 'Hi guys, in a hurry – must get my stuff and rush back to work ...' he said flying past them heading to his room. Nash seemed to leave things hanging in the air most of the time, then rushed around picking up the bits that made his life function as he needed them, so he was almost in perpetual motion it seemed.

'Heart of gold this guy but he could do with being a bit more together..' commented Andri loud enough so Nash could hear him. 'I heard that!' came the reply from the depth of Nash's room.

'Good!' answered Andri. 'I hope that means you will try to slow down one of these days ... while you still can.'

'Of course I will, don't you fret! See you guys later if you're around, I'm off work by six, so I'll swing by the house to see what's up ...' Nash's words were quickly covered by the sound of his footsteps crashing down the stairs.

'As I was saying,' continued Vincent slightly annoyed by the interruption, 'I think it's a dangerous thing. It keeps people thinking that they will be rewarded later for all the shit they have to go through this life, and to accept their lot – poverty, exploitation – rather than to question it. The spiritual life is now, here and now, not later. Christianity especially has worked well to keep the people subjugated in the so called third world, promising paradise, and throwing in hell just in case the incentive isn't big enough. The people are suffering, look at Nicaragua and El

Salvador, there is an uprising, they are trying to liberate themselves from what this government is doing down there, piss on their heads Reaganomics. And we, the westerners with some space to think about it all, we should be there helping, or at least out on the streets protesting against the fascism of America.' Vincent paused and then stood up. He walked to the bay window and cast his eyes over the big city stretching ahead of him.

'Oh, I couldn't agree more,' replied Andri. 'The whole thing about paradise and hell is designed to scare people into subjugation, and keep them obedient throughout their meek lives, whilst the likes of Mr. actor here pillage the resources of the countries helpless to defend themselves from this imperialism' – pointing to a poster on the wall of Regan wearing a king's gown adorned with nuclear missiles. 'In a way I think you are right, we should disregard the issue and just live in the present anyway. But it still is an important question, and . . .' Andri paused as he reviewed the evidence in his mind.

None of the people he knew to be dead had come back to tell him about it, so where did he get that belief from anyway? His grandmother on his mother's side had often described to him how she saw her mother's soul leave the body when she died, and how beautiful it was. And his other granny had told him about the vision she had three days after his grandfather's death. She'd apparently seen him, and he had talked to her to re-assure her that all was well and he was in a good place. His own spiritual experiences could be possibly explained in other ways, they didn't necessarily prove to him that there was life after death as such. And of course although he didn't doubt either of his grandmothers' accounts, they didn't prove anything either. 'The mind is strong, and the mind can create images, its own reality,' he thought out loud as his experiences with 'mentally ill' people he worked with came flashing in his mind to shore this conclusion in his brain.

'Exactly, the mind can play as many games as you like,' retorted Vincent. 'There's a protest rally being planned for the Spring down at the commons, all about Nicaragua and what's happening there. If you want to get involved with the organising let me know. Civil disobedience is going to be in the cards as well. Oh, yes and Noam Chomsky is doing a talk thing tomorrow, somewhere next to the library, Copley square – you know.'

'Hm? Oh yeah, I'll be coming to both surely . . .' replied Andri. Politics, spirituality, death. The concepts kept twisting in his mind like a concrete mix in a cement mixer, noisy and thick. He thought about the ghost dancers.

'Now here's a perplexing story . . .' he began to say but Vincent was already up and on the go with a '. . . catch you later, I'm on my way to meet Robin and some friends for a brew.'

'The story of the ghost dancers,' he continued to no-one there. Andri sat on the couch pondering the issues that had risen in his mind from the discussion with Vincent. He'd almost nodded off when the sound of someone scuffling about snapped him back to earth. 'Hello, hello!' came the voice of Thodoras who'd emerged from his room and popped his head in the living room to see who's about. 'What are you doing up so early?' he asked emphasising that he had just woken up with an accompanying yawn.

'Just got back from work. Been here for a while actually, Vincent and Nash are both out, don't know about Tom, haven't seen his face yet,' replied Andri shaking the dreamlike state from his head. 'Hey!' he exclaimed as if a revelation had just hit him 'I've got an interesting theological kind of issue to sift out, I think I'm onto something.'

Thodoras looked bemused. They often debated things, had done so for years now, and it usually involved some element of spirituality. Andri had a knack for using rationality to bolster any argument, whilst Thodoras had developed an equal knack of finding the holes in his reasoning. Inevitably their conversations were exploratory, not only because they both had a thirst for the 'truth' – whatever that may ever prove to be – but mainly because they both agreed on one thing, that they didn't know anything, so everything was open to interpretation and re-interpretation, very much the opposite of fundamentalist attitudes – no matter what the religion.

'So what's the big issue?' he asked looking around for his cigarettes.

'Well, I was having this conversation with Vincent earlier, about death, and the question of whether there is life after death, or whether the afterlife is an illusion with political roots – to control the people.' Andri paused in an effort to find that thread of thought that crossed his mind earlier in the day. 'Ah, yes,' he continued. 'The ghost dancers. You know the story. There was a first dance, after a Native American from the Pauite tribe, a guy called Wodziwob had a vision that the old tribal life would return, the dead would come back to life and the buffalo and other animals would be restored on the plains. The first ghost dance was held, a circle dance akin to the buffalo dance. Nothing much came out of it until a few years later, a child called Wovoka I think, again a Paiute, had a vision, and again like the first guy was transported to a higher realm – the spirit world – and was told that the dead would return, and their suffering would end if they danced this circle dance. He was even called the Indian messiah by the whites at the time, and soon they were all afraid of the tribes uniting under this new religion which promised the demise of the white man's world. So, on December 29 1890 the US army massacred them, over 300 people, men, women and children alike at Wounded Knee.' Andri paused and looked out of the window. The street looked cold and empty, complemented by the white snow and muddy ice covered sidewalks. It reminded him that many of the injured ghost dancers were left to die on the frozen snow. The image of Big Foot, a Lakota chief who'd camped with his people at Wounded Knee Creek the day before, his body frozen, arms reaching out was well imbedded in his memory.

'Yes, I know the history . . .' offered Thodoras 'so many massacres on this earth, so many wars . . . what's the insight?'

'Well, not an insight exactly, but listen me out. Here's a nation, subjugated, starved, persecuted. It wasn't the first time they had suffered, obviously, but this time their whole way of life was at the verge of collapse, of no return for the foreseeable future. So yes, in a way they were desperate for something to happen, which is why they took up the ghost dance so massively, I mean who in their right mind wouldn't want to get rid of the 'white man's civilisation' and bring back their long lost and many recently departed friends and relatives? But here's a culture which follows the visions of its people, let alone of a child from a shamanic lineage. The vision is the central way that Wakan Tanka – the Great Mystery – communicates with the people to give them guidance in times of need. Yet they are let down as the roll over of the white man's world did not happen, neither did the second coming, not yet anyway but they definitely expected all this to happen imminently. Instead they get massacred. And it got me thinking. I mean, it's easy to go down the one alternative path – that simply there is no God, no Wakan Tanka, and then visions are just some kind of wishful thinking, some utopian dream, a sweet in our mouth, something to suck on while we go through this one and only life, a chance occurrence that happened to produce me, you, and everything else that's living. So science would be the only valid body of knowledge, all else being the illusion. Ok, that much is easy. Now, consider for a minute that on the other end of the spectrum the truth is that say there is life after death, the spirit and some form of soul or some form of self consciousness survives the passage through death; that we come to this level of existence, physical manifestation, clothing ourselves with the earth, to learn and thus to grow and develop spiritually. And to complement this picture, since we are talking of native people's outlooks, that the basis of every life, every conscious being is love, and the one unifying principle that everything is part of one consciousness, that of God. In this case then, it seems inconceivable that the Great Spirit would give them a false vision, more likely that it was interpreted wrongly.'

'Sure, it's a possibility.' said Thodoras thoughtfully. 'The present civilisation will come to an end eventually -that much is inevitable. They might have misread the bit about when it would all happen, after all if someone asks you to revolt now in the knowledge that your actions would have an effect many generations after you die, you'd probably not bother. Anyway this second coming business, whether we are talking about the Native Americans and ghost dancing, or White Buffalo Calf Woman, or we're talking the Christ thing, Revelations, end of the world kind of stuff, could all be the sweetened pill as you said. Some say it will all happen in 2000, some – like the Mayans say 2012. I suppose if we're alive then we'll find out, but until then . . .'

'Ok, the when, and if is of course unknown. But, on the other hand, why give people a vision if there is no point of carrying it through? Regardless of the when, it must have had a meaning to do the dance, maybe it still has. Because, if you believe like they did that by dancing the spirit world would open up in this dimension, then the dance is more than symbolic, more than a theatre for learning purposes, it's actually *a channel through which reality changes*. There is some kind of alchemy involved. And if Wakan Tanka, the Great Mystery, God or however you want to call that which created and is in everything, gave them such a vision, and it is going to happen some day, wouldn't it be unfair if the ghost dancers weren't here to experience that? Wouldn't they have to be present?' Andri paused and reflected on that last thought. He was talking about re-incarnation, something of which he had always been far from convinced of.

'That's more of a Buddhist concept there than Native American,' commented Thodoras. He'd been always intrigued by the spiritual, and now his studies in journalism and theology had given him the perfect opportunity to focus on his favourite subjects – much to the dismay of his father who'd prefer to see him doing something down to earth such as accounting. 'Second coming yes, Native American and Christian, but re-incarnation? As far as I know, although they do believe in the spirit world and the spirits of their ancestors, they also believe that when you die your essence is dissipated around the earth and that's that. Finito. The end.'

'Well yes, on second thought I actually agree with you there, another dead end. Food for thought anyway. Hey, Noam Chomsky is giving a talk tomorrow, downtown – interested?' Andri said as he got up to go to the kitchen.

'But of course! I was planning to go to that,' replied Thodoras getting another cigarette from the pack.

CHAPTER 6

WASHINGTON'S STATUE

It was early May and spring was well underway. The winter snow had melted away, mostly gathered by the Charles River and all its tributaries and some taken up in the air in preparation of the gathering springtime rains. The varied bulbs in the parks and street verges had broken through and had been flowering for a while now, accompanied by the start of the tree blossom, apple and cherry being the most common. It was a warm sunny day, just right for a peace rally to express solidarity with the people of El Salvador and Nicaragua and to protest about the active involvement of the US government, secret services and military on the side of the totalitarian puppet regimes there.

Vincent had riled everyone up, and after the usual ritualistic delays of the morning, including numerous coffees and cigarettes, they all piled in the subway on the red line for downtown Boston. The train was packed with people on the way to the protest march. There was a good mix of ages, including families with young children and a good deal of retired citizens, including some that looked to have been on every protest march that ever happened, and some might well have been! The largest group however was in their late teens and early twenties – students in the many universities around the metropolis, with a mix of attitudes from the peacefully subdued to the rearing to get wild. The amount of placards and rolled up cloth banners made the clear distinction between this crowd going to a protest march rather than a baseball game.

Every station closer to downtown the crowds got bigger, and the platforms were full to the brim. Thodoras suggested they got off a stop before the rally and walk through the commons, the gardens there being a much better alternative than the crowded subway. A minute later they all came off the train which was close to bursting at the seams and after a concerted push through the oncoming crowds found themselves out in the fresh air.

'Boy I couldn't stand it much longer in that sardine can,' admitted Felipe as they strolled past the busy diners outside the station. Thodoras nodded whilst lighting a cigarette. After a short debate whether they should stop at a bar for a quick beer and deciding it was too early and they should have their wits about, they walked over the hillside to the north side of the gardens. Mother Nature blazed through the red brick 18th century houses, its presence soothing yet wild in spite of the constant efforts of the city gardeners to keep it absolutely orderly and managed. The group rambled along taking in the colours and smells of spring, past the statute of Washington on his horse, the patches of red tulips and the swan lake with the old weeping willow trees. The Park was on the other side, and the march was going to pass next to it, approaching from the Haymarket and past the old city cemetery.

'This is where it's going to happen,' announced Vincent pointing at the far corner of the Park. 'My friends and I will be taking over the street there, squatting until we're arrested and carried away! Civil Disobedience, the rightful expression of the people's anger,' he added. 'This is democracy in action, this is doing something about it, so are you guys coming?'

Andri didn't hesitate to answer 'I don't know about the rest of you, but I don't see much point in getting arrested. I'm not putting you down for it, just not my thing. I'm going to walk around the march and do something spontaneous, I'm sure I'll think of something.' He wasn't being apologetic, just honest. That's the way he felt about it, and Vincent surely knew that. Thodoras and Nash decided to stay with Andri. The rest of the group waved goodbye and followed Vincent to join in with the crowds.

The cops had taken positions early on, they'd seen them from the hillside, another reason they all had agreed to get off the train a stop early. Thodoras was moving about taking photos and notes in his pocket journal, and Nash had hooked up with some folks he knew from work, so he was going to meet them later. Andri joined the march for a short distance then watched from the sidelines as the sea of people ebbed and flowed. The civil disobedience had begun, and the police had already started to drag some people away and into the vans, which were parked all around the side streets together with groups of riot cops. Andri smirked, remembering Gary, someone he met earlier that year whilst on the quest for mescaline. Thodoras had introduced him; they'd met in the 24 hour shop where Andri and Thodoras worked on the graveyard shift. He seemed like a good enough guy, not entirely there but he'd turned them on to some good weed, and boasted of being able to get some mescaline, which was becoming a rare commodity in the city. He lived in a basement flat, somewhere in Somerville on the hills. One evening, after a long hunt through the dark back alleys of Charlestown and negotiations with some shady individuals, Thodoras and Andri had found themselves in Gary's flat, looking at some dubious pills that Gary insisted was mescaline. They'd had a few beers and Thodoras had opened the closet by mistake whilst looking for the toilet only to discover a riot police outfit.

'A souvenir?' Thodoras had asked hopefully.

'Oh, no just my part time job. It's crazy, they don't want us working locally, in case we have to beat up someone we know, so they ship us out all over the place – mostly around Chicago and Detroit, you know workers union strikes and such trouble. We go there, Yaaaaaaa! Crash! Bang! Smash some heads open, and a couple days later they fly us back home. The money is good though, pays for the beer and more,' had come the shocking reply. Thodoras and Andri had looked at each other in disbelief and burst out laughing as Gary sipped on his Adolphus Miller lite beer. What perfect irony! And to top it all they were certain that Gary had no idea about A Miller, or anything remotely political for that matter as they'd found out by pointing out that bashing people's head in isn't exactly a healthy way to make a living, not to mention it could seriously damage the person on the receiving end.

But Gary wasn't about to change, unlike themselves he wasn't on a journey of self discovery. He'd knit his life well, all stitched up including his recreational drugs – for the pretty colours and other amusing effects- and the part time job to pay for it. Andri couldn't help wondering where these riot cops were from, probably Detroit he thought.

The march was gathering momentum, and by now the civil disobedience had taken its toll on everyone else involved apart from the protestors, who were high on the disobedience rush – here and now! – and were chanting away joyfully. The cops had started becoming a bit more rough in their handling in spite of the media presence which was waiting for any shots of a bloody shirt, a risen baton or other glamorous act of violence. A few streets over there was even more action, as some fringe elements were doing their thing, trying to instil some reaction from the cops by throwing stones and bottles at them.

'Things are warming up,' Thodoras voice came from behind him. Andri turned and raised his arm instinctively as Thodoras pressed on the camera shutter. 'Yeah, well . . .' replied Andri. 'Have they arrested Vince yet?' he asked.

'I don't think so, I've been taking pictures of the action but I didn't see him being dragged. I lost him at some point, but some protestors have moved further back and are trying to start something,' he replied.

'Yeah, I've seen them. It's all so tame though, in comparison . . .' he muttered. Back in Greece, only a few years earlier, they were running around the streets of Athens during the people's uprising against the US backed military dictatorship, the Junta as it was known. The uprising was sparked off by the students who took over the buildings of the Athens Polytechnic, soon to be joined by masses of people and become a popular uprising that lasted for days and which became the beginning of the end of the seven year dictatorship. He was barely a teenager then, but with his friends still very aware of what was going down. Most everyone knew of someone who had vanished, arrested and tortured by the brutal military police. So when the time came they were out on the streets in a flash. Petroleum jelly around the eyes and a cloth over the nose for the teargas. Rioters were burning tyres all over the streets to disperse the gas, which was being launched in the riot police counter attacks, a game of cat and mouse that was being played in the streets. The crowds proved too massive however for the riot police alone to control, thousands of people amassed around the Polytechnic, protecting the fire of freedom that burned there. The students had set up a crude radio transmitter, and had organised all functions of life within the grounds in a temporary but well functioning anarchist utopia. The battles with the riot police ebbed and flowed through the nights.

On the fourth day the tanks arrived. The earth was shaking from their rumbling approach. The characteristic clattering sound of the chains of a tank manoeuvring through a city is one anyone who has been fleeing from them would never forget, and Andri certainly hadn't. He'd first heard that sound over six years earlier, when the tanks first rolled into Athens to establish the beginning of the Junta. The loud clattering noise was soon followed by the tap tapping sound of bullets from the mounted machine guns hitting the rendered brick walls of the city's tall buildings, blasting chunks of brick and mortar over their heads as they ran for cover. Back at his friend's basement they listened to the student transmission 'Radio of Free Greece' as the commentator described the entrance of the tanks into the Polytechnic. The radio went quiet. Many died that day, 17th of November 1973.

'Hmm? Tame, well yes, thank God for that! This is civilised, a tea party in comparison to other parts of the world. Still, better than nothing!' he said smiling. 'I remember, you was a staunch Marxist back then,' he added.

'Yeah, we read our Marx and Engle, and the little red book of Mao. But I soon got over it, once I realised the party members were just as bad as the fascists, in fact had they replaced them things wouldn't be much different in essence. The two extremes meet, like in a loop. Anyway, let's get out of here,' suggested Andri making a move away from the action. 'I think it's time for a truly symbolic act, and I've got a good idea what to do.' He started up the road on the outside of the park that run up the hill past the golden domed Capitol towards the Commons. Right behind the first buildings next to the park they noticed the mounted police, waiting by their big strong horses for the final call, the last piece of the action whatever and whenever, because when they rolled in things usually got pretty messy. On the way they encountered Nash, who'd hooked up with Vincent and his group and had decided not to get busted yet, so they all meandered into the gardens.

'Look around you, what do you see?' asked Andri gesturing with his arm. 'The march is going on, the protesters are blocking the road and being carted away, and the cops are basically monitoring it all. Well, here,' he said pointing to the bigger than life statue of Washington, 'we have an opportunity. We can take over Washington's statue, what could be more symbolic? He fought for freedom and so are we. We stand by his principles, whether he likes it or not . . . and wave our banners,' he'd hardly finished talking when Vincent pulled himself up the tall base and had attached a banner which read 'Nicaragua Libre! US out!' on the general's drawn out sword. 'Bread not Bombs' and 'Save the Earth' were soon attached. In no time the statue was full of people, and soon other protesters who had been wandering about joined them with drums and rattles and more banners. The takeover lasted a few hours, during which people came and went, sang and danced and taunted the mounted cops who had shown up a couple of times and chased them around, but had probably decided it wasn't worth hassling with, so eventually left them to it. At nightfall the march had long ended, and the few remaining crowds were dispersing into the shadows. The group had managed to hold their ground and make their statement and headed back to the house.

'We've made our point and had our fun as well,' said Andri as a parting note looking back to the statue as they were leaving.

'Yeah, but we didn't manage to get arrested!' exclaimed Thodoras. They all laughed.

CHAPTER 7
THE SCUZZYWOMP

'Scuzzy what?' Asked Penny in her giggly laughing way.

'Scuzzy-womp. Its scuzzy – muddy that is – and we're womping through the woods, with our big backpacks pulling us this way and that!' replied Andri in an equally good mood.

It was a favourite activity for most of them, camping far out there in the wilderness. The far out there aspect was important, as some of their favourite haunts were close to well travelled paths, and areas quite popular in the peak summer months. This fact, and the sheer joy of discovering new magical spots had led them to travel further North this time. They were well on the trail now, having gone through the 'where is this damn trailhead anyway?' and 'are you sure it's this way', and the rest of it, usual elements of decompression from the big metropolis to the 'great outdoors'. The smells of the forest, the muffling of the sound from the blanket of leaves, that vibrant moisture in the air that tells you you're inside something alive and breathing, the feeling of home stronger than anywhere else. Andri had always felt the forest his home, more than any other natural or artificial environment. It wasn't any one element that made him feel that way, the trees, or animals, the rocks, ferns, or creeks. It was the feeling of the oneness of it all, the clarity of what creation's intention is, and the miracle of its workings that did it for him. That feeling that he was part of this one huge and sacred being, this never ending circle of light.

'I like it, it even sounds like a tribal name, so let's call our little tribe *the Scuzzywomps*!' exclaimed Kevin and he started chanting something that sounded like a native American chant. 'Hey-ya, hey-ya, Scuzzy-Womp!' The 'old mule' as he called himself on similar occasions, was a good hiker, moving along faster than most in spite of the fact he was the eldest of the group.

'There's a spring coming up, and according to the map it's the last one for a while, until we're almost at the campsite, so better stock up folks,' said James. He was studying the map whilst holding it with his left hand, compass on the right, and still leading the way up the path. 'In fact here it is,' he said pointing to the spring on the right of the trail. This came as no surprise to anyone, as he was an experienced woodsman, who seemed to know all you ever needed to live in nature.

They were starting to ascend now, having left the forest floor for the past half mile. The trail ran on the south western side of the mountain, so they could see the valley with the river running through it on the left as they went up. The sound of the river went from a strong rushing sound to a soft faraway cascading melody as it slowly dropped out of view behind the thick forest growth. In spite of their best efforts, and all the planning and packing in the past days, the group still started off from the trail-head late in the morning, and having trekked for a few hours already were facing the prospect of getting there in the dark.

'Great. It looks like were going to be looking for wood in the dark to make a fire,' said Thodoras, jokingly showing his dissatisfaction with the whole process as he reached for his flashlight. 'I want this on my belt now that I can still find it,' he whispered, as if divulging some big secret.

Sure enough the group looked like a bunch of aliens landing in the night when they arrived at the camp, beams of light from the flashlights streaming through the trees. This was one of many trips they had taken in the woods together, forming on the way a tribal awareness of some sort that kept on surprising them with more gifts in the form of high experiences. They were all wandering about, each doing their thing in their own way, gathering wood, water, setting up tarps, kitchen and all the other little things that make life better in the woods. Soon the fire was roaring, the stew was well on its way and most tents had been set up, ready for the night. Thodoras was helping Nash with some bigger tarps, James was de-mucking some of his gear whilst tending the fire, and Kevin and Penny were stumbling about and laughing in the dark picking some more wood. Andri gave the stew another stir. 'Almost ready now,' he said turning to James. 'I suppose we should smoke a pipe now,' he said in a jokingly ceremonial way, his arm lost in his backpack scrambling about for something. 'Aha, here it is! The implement of thy smoke!' he said laughingly as he pulled out a cherry wood pipe in the shape of a corkscrew. He'd made the pipe himself, one of many. He loved working with wood and making things with it, and found he could immerse himself in pipe making for hours on end, drilling, carving, shaping and sanding. It all seemed to happen all at once, but in fact it could take days or even weeks from start to finish as there was a necessary connection that had to be achieved first, between the wood and the hand. Once the hand had communicated with the wood, the image of the pipe would appear in his head, and from that point on he couldn't get his hands off it until it was finished.

'Yohimbe!' The cry of the Scuzzywomps echoed through the trees as they all gathered around the fire and passed the pipe around. The summoning cry for the smoking of the pipe had emerged from working with other crews on a big renovation job, out of necessity so to say as they needed a code word which the rest on the site didn't understand. Now yohimbe is a substance recently discovered and derived from a tree in Africa, and it has the effect of giving an erection, so it was a bit of a joke amongst the group. The food was ready, and soon they were all sitting around polishing the pot.

'Interesting how food tastes so much better when you are out in nature,' said Kevin.

'Mmmm, yes. Must be all this fresh air,' said Nash, 'opens the nostrils ... pass some of that pitta bread, that's really good warmed up on a hot rock, just like this ... here have some,' he said passing the warm bread around. Soon the small feast had ended and the cleanup was taking place.

It was Thodoras inadvertently banging the pots together as he was cleaning them that sparked it. Not that the rest needed any big excuse to start making noise. Kevin caught up straight away by picking up two stones and playing percussion along the banging. Penny disappeared for a while and then came out of her tent with a large wooden recorder, a bass. Andri produced his wooden treble recorder, while Nash went for the chanting. In the meantime, James had been busy not only stocking the fire but also amassing an impressive number of different sounding pieces of wood, stones and pinecones making a sort of percussion rack and mounting the rest of the cooking pots, pans and ladles on it. Stomping on the forest floor provided the earth drum and soon the sounds of jungle beat were spontaneously erupting through the leafy canopy of the dark woods. It was a clear night with few solitary clouds in the sky travelling past as if only to point out the enormous distance of the stars studded on the inner belly of the great black panther.

The music was arriving at a crescendo, the waves piling up to each other and pushing the crest higher and higher. The earth was warm and vibrating responding in kind to the primal event that was taking place, a human expression unaltered for thousands of years, the reaction of the soul to the awe inspired to it by Mother Nature, the joy of Her welcome embrace. Andri was deeply immersed in this Oneness, head back all the way blowing on the recorder. He could feel the wind welling from the bottom of his spine and gushing straight up through him, through his neck and mouth and through the wooden instrument in a straight line extending past the tall pine trees into the sky.

He felt the line of energy extending in both directions, all the way from the very centre of the Earth to the stars above him. The line slowly became a tunnel a few feet wide, a tunnel of blue light, a shower of incredibly bright tiny stars raining through him.

The morning Sun peered through the haziness of the low clouds that had rolled in just before dawn. It was going to be a steep climb to the peak, and the low visibility meant a slower, riskier ascent. Walking off the mountain wasn't uncommon, and one had to veer off the track only a few feet to find him or her self lost in a dangerous landscape. You don't have to fall a few thousand feet to die, just a couple will do if you get stranded and exposed to the changing weather overnight. There were enough of them to feel safe in most conditions, they just had to keep track of each other. They hadn't brought ropes, so a chain was going to have to depend on each other's vigilance and eyesight. A couple of mugs full of coffee and some forest pancakes later and the Scuzzywomps were on their way. The events of the night had added some sticks and feathers to their day packs, and leaving the base camp they looked more like a pack of nomads from some futuristic film rather than twentieth century hikers.

The trail was ablaze with the reflection of the myriad tiny quartz crystals mixed with layers of mica that seemed to form a carpet through the solid granite outcrops. It wended up for a couple of miles, gradually getting steeper, but still easy to trek without using hands. The map showed a couple of approaches to the summit. They'd taken James's advice to use the longer approach over the lower peak and across the saddle ridge to the summit, avoiding the shorter but steeper route.

'It's much safer,' insisted James. 'Anyway, we need to warm up before we get to the last climb, it looks quite steep on the map and they are accurate these maps. There're some caves up there I hear, the guide says the approach is "treacherous and obscured by dense growth", so I don't expect we'll find them. The summit it's said is magical, pity about the fog though.'

'It could well clear up for us,' replied Kevin in an unusually optimistic way. 'The sun will soon burn out the clouds, thin and transient they are like us.' Kevin considered himself a cynic, if anything, masquerading his disillusionment after the 60s with a layer of intellectual anarchy and a sometimes hardened entrenchment in the belief that no good was going to come out of humanity. When it came to art however he let himself rip, expressing deep pagan roots and a vibrant spirit. In the city he worked as a glass bender for a small neon light business, wrote poetry, made aboriginal looking paintings and played rock and roll. But in the woods he seemed much older and wiser.

By the time the group had reached the steep ascent the clouds were still very present. It was too risky to explore for the caves, so they decided to press on. There was very little soil for plants to grow as they were now close to the peak and the terrain was mostly left to the exposed grey granite outcrops. The going was hard now and they stuck together as a group by calling out in sequence so they could tell if anyone strayed off the path. The sounds that came out spontaneously although varied all sounded tribal and duly apt to the surrounding environment. They stopped only once, to gather and make sure all were accounted for, and to prepare a hot drink on one of James's foldable camping stoves. The wind was picking up, and the stove proved a bit of a challenge, rectified after James decided to give it a good clean, and ended up taking it apart and re-assembling it, which only took a short while and a quick pass of the pipe.

The summit seemed to jump at them for they didn't realise they were there until the last few yards as it was concealed by the fog. The wind was blowing strong now, and the fast moving clouds offered glimpses of lush valleys far below in the distance. It was approaching mid day and the sun was surely doing its job as Kevin predicted. Slowly but surely it was clearing out. Right on the summit was a strange formation of large granite outcrops, in a layout that seemed almost perfect. There were two equal sized and shaped huge boulders in the middle, sticking out of the ground for a few feet and forming a square space in between. On the one side of the one boulder and the other side of the other were another six boulders of decreasing size. They all gathered in between the two big boulders, and after a brief circle decided it would be the perfect place to light a fire and warm up from the wind. It would have to be a small fire, the peak was quite nude and had only a few small twigs to offer. Soon it was all ready to go, a small pile of wood expertly set up and half a dozen experienced campers around it. James went first in the attempt to light it. They all knew it was going to be a difficult task, the summit was exposed and the wind howling relentlessly. None the less they were surprised when James gave up, having seen him on more than one occasion lighting fires in the pouring rain. The wind was getting the better of them however, and one by one they all failed to do what each one thought they could.

'This aint gonna work,' muttered Andri whist James had another go at the fire.

'Well I'm not surprised with all this wind, it's damn impossible!' Nash's words were taken by the wind as he uttered them.

'No, we're doing something wrong, the approach isn't doing it,' replied Andri. 'I think it's because we're not trying together, we are a circle after all and this is a highly symbolic fire. Let's just do this . . . everyone squat around the wood pile in a circle, and we'll throw the last match in and all stand up at once. That's the signal that we want the fire to rise – what'd you say? Shall we try it?'

'I'm all for it, it's getting cold up here,' came the whisper from Penny. She was huddled up with Jackie, a friend of Kevin's from the Dakotas who was visiting Boston with the outlook of settling. Kevin nodded, James lit the match and they all looked at each other and stood up together. Almost the same instance a large flame jumped out through the wood, and in seconds the wind had fanned it into a roaring fire. They all stood there speechless for quite a while. Jackie broke the silence first.

'Wow! That was just amazing! Did you see that, did you see what happened there? I don't know what you guys are used to, but that's something . . .' She looked around the circle inquisitively. Andri could see the doubt building up in her eyes.

'Yes, we saw it,' he replied, reassuringly nodding his head. 'Stuff like that does tend to happen on these trips, it's the tribal thing working.'

The intense fire had all but died out having burnt the small twigs they'd managed to gather from the slopes. The Sun had by now also burnt out the low clouds, the wind dispersing what was left, and for the first time since the assent they could see the whole summit and the valleys below. Now the fire had gone they started moving about and soaking in the rays. The big granite boulders they had seen at first where not standing there alone. It turns out there were patterns of rock on the two other directions, north and south, the one in the north coming to a triangular formation, the pattern in the south spreading out like a fan. Andri and James climbed up on one of the biggest boulders to take the whole thing in.

'Amazing! And you could almost miss it in the fog! And yet it's so clear.' said Andri.

'Yes, I agree, I've never seen a natural formation of rock that resembles an eagle so much as this. There's the head, there's the tail,' he said pointing to the triangle and the fan shaped outcrops, 'and the ones we saw first are the wings. And there! Look down there towards the valley!' James grabbed Andri by the shoulder and spun him around to face the eagles soaring in the distant thermals. Three of them circling in the clear blue sky, powerful, free.

The rest of the hike was relatively uneventful. They stayed on the peak for a while, enjoying the sunlight and sharing some food. By nightfall they'd reached the base camp and sat around the fire subdued. It was an early night for most, soon in their sleeping bags and snoring away the day's hardship. Thodoras was poking the fire to get a better view of the deep orange coals in the centre. A loud crashing sound broke the silence and Nash soon emerged cursing from behind some thick brush dragging a small tree.

'Damn fucking pots! Who put them there anyway?' he complained.

'You did, after dinner,' replied Thodoras still focused on the fire.

'Oh yes, I put them there to dry. Well they're dry now! I'll pick them up in the morning when I can see what I'm doing. Anyway, here,' he said dragging the tree next to the fire. 'Dead standing, nice and dry. This will last us a while.' He sat on a log close to Thodoras who seemed to be in his own world. 'How about something to warm us up? I've got a bit of brandy here,' he said pulling a small metal flask from the big side pocket on his trousers. He took a good swig and passed it over to Thodoras who was deep in thought. Thodoras took a swig and passed the bottle back to Nash. 'Thanks, that is good,' he said.

'Hm, yeah. So what's up Theo, what you thinking about? Women?' Nash knew Thodoras could be very withdrawn. He often wondered if so much introspection could be bad for you. He liked to analyse things too, of course, but his nature was much more outgoing, so he'd soon focus out. While Thodoras, he could coil up for days and speak to no one. And women, well in his life they always seemed to go hand in hand with problems, although he couldn't pretend he minded, life was full of problems and he couldn't keep away from them anyway!

'No, not women, although now you mention it Jackie seems like a nice girl,' Thodoras looked towards her tent instinctively and was relieved that there were no signs of life coming from there. He wouldn't have wanted her to overhear him. Nash chuckled.

'Oh she's definitely a woman not a girl. And I'm quite sure James fancies her, he certainly pays a lot of attention to her needs!' he said. 'So what is on your mind?' he insisted.

'I wish I knew. I guess I'm sick of it, all the wars. I grew up in wars, all my childhood there would be something going on. As a kid you just take it all in, the pain the sorrow, the tears the hunger. People whom you knew just disappear, one day they're there the next gone. Adults and children alike. Even the animals suffer, it's not nice being bombed. And the bastards who run the show, a bunch of gangsters. They control so much, and keep on taking ever more out of the earth, out of people. There seems no end to it, and no way to stop them as they destroy the planet and us with it.'

'Yeah, I know,' replied Nash in a lower tone than earlier. 'But we live in hope that things will change, cause if we don't and we just give up then nothing will change. That's when they've won.'

'"I hope for nothing. I fear nothing. I'm free," Seferis, a contemporary Greek poet,' replied Thodoras. 'And in any case, "us and them" isn't supposed to be a good way of looking at things. It mixes hatred and other negatives in there, and after all "they" are victims of themselves as well. And politics? Representative democracy my ass! All the politicians represent is the big companies, the economic interests which rule unimpeded. Oh they plot and they plan ... and God is supposed to plot and plan better than them, so where is it?'

'Ah, we're getting somewhere,' interrupted Nash. 'I have no answer to that, but isn't it too soon to judge since we still haven't arrived at the end, Armageddon?'

'Yes, I suppose, if you believe in that kind of thing. In the mean time people are getting slaughtered and are dying of poverty related deaths all over the globe. In comparison we live the lives of kings. And yet we have no power to change things.'

'Not convinced by Vincent then? Nor am I,' said Nash, scratching his scraggly beard. Vincent was the political activist of the group. He wasn't much into the tribal experience, although he was well accustomed to living outdoors, it's just that he chose to 'vacation' in central America with a group of activists helping those in need to rebuild their lives. Nash, like the rest of them, applauded his friend's altruism, but didn't share his optimism.

'Sure, he's got a point, and I will go to the peace march, it's just that I don't think anything will change because of it. So a few people are exposed to it, and their eyes are opened a little. So what? And what we all do to stop what's going on? Get arrested for squatting on the road and blocking traffic? Big deal!'

'Well, it's better than waiting for a miracle to happen, isn't it?' asked Nash. He got up from the log and snapped some branches off the dead tree and threw them in the fire. The hot coals were hungry and the flames soon shot up illuminating the trees along the clearing in the woods they'd chosen for the base camp. The air was still, and apart from the crackling of the pine needles in the fire little else could be heard. Occasionally some large animal, moose or bear, would pass close enough to the camp to make their presence known and then wander off, but none came too close.

'Maybe it is something to keep you thinking there is hope, but hope can be false. And you live your life, a slave to the system which dangles TVs, cars and all sorts in front of your face, and you get old proud of how good your washing machine is, and how fast your car is and all that. An empty life full of lies. What's the point? And if they got you convinced that if you go to church every Sunday you'll go to heaven then you're a blind fool as well!' Thodoras carefully placed his tobacco pouch on his knees and rolled another cigarette.

'You Greeks! Always philosophising like your forefathers!' said Nash. 'I don't disagree with all that, but I still think your existential problems would bother you less if you had a good woman in bed with you.' Thodoras smiled. 'I'm going to hit the sack Theo, you take it easy. Now where's that flashlight, oh here it is . . .' Nash scrambled into his tent and after what sounded like a symphony of zippers opening and closing he was soon competing for the loudest base camp snore. Thodoras fixed his eyes on the coals and pulled a half burned branch off the fire to light his cigarette.

CHAPTER 8
BOY MEETS WIZARD

He closed his eyes and tried to remember. For a long time nothing happened. Then he heard an owl 'hoot, hoot' circling above his head. The sound was deep and sharp, overcoming any other sounds and piercing the stillness of the mind, the air shimmering and vibrating in front of him, like a piece of fabric where someone had hung the stars on, waving in the wind. Through the mist of anticipation and tiredness an image of a gate emerged. He approached it slowly and slipped through to the other side, tuning in – looking out. Darkness. He felt weightless. Was he floating in the void? It almost felt like that, apart from his feet. They were definitely touching something; it felt soft and warm. His eyes had started adjusting to the light, it felt like dawn. Looking down he realised he was wearing moccasins. There was some beadwork, some sort of gold, red and black bird in a blue circle. It had something like a tiny white cross in the middle. The next thing he noticed was his hands. They were his all right, but somehow different. It slowly sunk in that he was a child again.

Suddenly, he was there, with no recollection of adulthood. A child wearing soft skin moccasins, walking gently on the Earth. The moccasins seemed to float on the soft bed of pine needles, as the young boy walked through the trees with almost no sound but a faint shuffling. The pines were getting smaller and shorter, so he knew he was now close to the edge of the forest, where the climb gets steeper, on the rocky mountainside. Clearing the last trees, he faced a rock wall, and on the top part of the rock a tall castle, its base growing out of the rock itself like some tree fungus, and with pointy narrow towers piercing the clouds.

He started climbing. He could feel the rock but was also aware he wasn't touching it. It was a feeling he was familiar with, like walking in a dream, only he was totally awake, and definitely in his body, or so it seemed. Caught in the spirit of a mountain goat, led by Innocence herself in the body of a child he swiftly moved along the foot wide narrow path catching the wind swivelling between the rocks, heart beating a silent drum. As he floated almost effortlessly up towards the castle he knew now he was out of his physical body, but the thought was quickly pushed aside by the more pressing concern of getting in the castle, which had no apparent gate or door. The ancient building was enclosed in the mountain's solid rock hug, shadows playing, mystifying, on the round stone walls. He climbed around to the less visible eastern side of the outer wall, where he discovered a small window, with two thick iron bars crossing each other, but no glass.

'Perfect,' he thought, 'I can squeeze through here if I try,' so he stuck his head through and then he was in. On the inside of the window there was a small ledge, and he perched there his eyes adjusting to the dim light. It felt like he was up high, close to the ceiling of a big tall room, only he couldn't quite see the floor. The room was round and square and of many shapes all in one instance ever-changing. Suddenly there was a bright flash of light, rising from the middle of the floor and filling the room with a clear blue light. The light looked like it was sparkling in all directions, like lightning but not as frightening. In fact the light was warm, and it warmed his soul like a mother's kiss. Down there he could now discern the source of the flash, a white haired man with a long white beard, wearing a cloak and a pointed hat, both blue with stars and moons on it shimmering like the real thing. A sphere of white light was floating on the peak of the conical hat. The wizard was moving his arms about and chanting something incomprehensible with a lot of Aaas and Ooos. Every now and then he would bring his hands together as if to clap and a flash of light would spark off and fill the room with its magic light. The wizard started swirling faster and faster, the chanting blending into a whirling sound that was getting louder and louder until it exploded into all and every possible colour all at once completely filling the space around it. He looked down and saw the wizard still dancing.

'He's doing some ritual or something. What if he sees me? I could be in serious trouble here.' No sooner than the thought had occurred to him, he noticed turning his head up to the right that the wizard was there on the perch with him, looking down on him. He looked down, bewildered how he could have snuck up on him so quickly, and realised that down there, the wizard was still dancing!

'But, how..?' he started to mutter turning back to the presence next to him who just smiled and covered him with his cloak.

☯

He ran in the darkness, afraid of being caught. In a dark corridor he found a door, opened it and slipped in quietly, feeling certain the wizard was somewhere around the room, which was filled with glass tubes of all shapes, bottles with fluids and gases shimmering like the moon light. He turned and saw a table with toys on it, and a frame with curtains pulled, like a theatre stage for tiny people, a doll of a magician child dressed in a shimmering gold robe, pointed round hat full of stars.

Next thing he knew he was in a library, still in the castle he felt. In front of him a huge wooden table, and on the other side the wizard, still smiling at him. He couldn't quite focus on the table, and he sensed something was not right.

'Yes, but can you tell what it is?' As the wizard spoke, his voice sounded very familiar. He couldn't quite place his voice, but he realised straight away that he had read his mind. The answer came, even before the thought occurred to him.

'Yes, I can. I do know you better than you know yourself after all. Now look not towards me, but to the other end of the table.'

The little boy turned his head to his left. There was something wrong about the table all right, it had no end!

'It has no end!' he exclaimed, almost chocking himself

in disbelief. He turned around to the right, this time half expecting the shock, and indeed there was no end there either.

'Now compare the two sides of the table, on your left, where you first looked, and the right, where you looked to confirm or reject what you just saw.' The wizard's voice was clear, but it wasn't very clear where it was coming from. Still, it had a very familiar quality, and felt all together reassuring.

'I suppose there is no end to this table either side, but "no end" seems shorter on the right,' said the boy.

'You see well,' said the wizard in approval. 'The reason for the difference is in your mind. Having seen that which has no end, your mind creates a shortcut, which allows you to recognise the endless more quickly, giving the illusion of being a bit closer. Although your mind knows it isn't rational, after all no end means just that and so the two should be just as far, your experience is that one is closer than the other. And indeed it is, because you have looked at it, seen it and somehow changed it,' he said. His voice instigated a reassuring sensation, revealing a depth of knowledge and clarity of intention.

'But what's the truth? Are they the same, or is it just the way I think about it?' asked the boy, starting to get confused now.

'You've answered that one yourself already. They are the same and different at the same time. Both your rational conclusion that they are the same, and your sensory experience of it that they are slightly different are correct simultaneously,' answered the wizard. He let his words hang in the air in some magical kind of way, that reminded the boy of the light show he had just experienced, or had he? Doubt started creeping in. He had to say it, as his mind nagged his tongue to move.

'But that's impossible, the two contradict each other!' he exclaimed.

'Perception is like a door to another world,' said the wizard. 'You can open it and look through, or you can step over the threshold and experience it up close. When you are in, things look different than when you were out looking in, because awareness isn't limited any more to what you can see with the mind, but instead it includes all the other senses as well. Once the mind accepts the possibility of something, it opens up to it on many levels. If your mind cannot accept the possibility, then you don't see it at all, although it's there all the time. Look for example at the table right in front of you now. Don't turn your head, but just focus on the surface of it, and recall the two ends of it and how they are the same but different.'

The boy focused his eyes on the surface in front of him. The wood surface was dark, and shiny, almost like a very still lake with ripples that had suddenly been frozen in mid motion. The surface glistened and there seemed to be very tiny lights shimmering on it.

'Feel how thick the table really is, look beyond the surface as if it were transparent to you,' said the wizard. He seemed to be closer now, almost next to him. The boy looked more intently. There was some distant sound in his ears, floating about. The wizard was chanting, although that seemed to come from far away; his vision started to blur ever so slightly. He couldn't tell how much time had passed since he first looked at the table, but suddenly he felt as if he was leaning on something which gave way. In front of him the table felt very deep; in fact it felt as if there was no end to its depth. The tiny lights on the surface had grown into big massive stars, and the boy found himself floating in the night sky amongst them.

'Here, hold on to my hand,' offered the wizard who seemed to be stretching out from afar, and as soon as the boy touched his hand he found himself perched on the side of the mountain on a huge granite outcrop. He found himself sitting on the edge and instinctively shuffled his body back from what looked like an endless drop. He could see no path or possible approach to this place from below. Behind him were a few short trees and bushes and the entrance to a cave at the foot of another steep outcrop to the top of the mountain. The old man appeared next to him. He looked different, younger somehow, wearing some sort of animal hide, feathers tied on his hair.

'How did we get here?' asked the boy.

'We've been here all along,' said the old man. 'You have been here before, a long long time ago, to this very cave,' he said pointing at the entrance which was closer now. 'But this time you are here because you need to be with the eagles, so follow me,' he said and climbed on the westerly side of the cave, up what looked to the eye as an impossible climb. Although the little boy knew that all this he was experiencing in his other body, he was still afraid some harm might come to him if he fell, so he hesitated and slipped. The wizard caught his arm and pulled him up. 'You are right to be afraid, for there is danger here, but don't hesitate, for that would be the most dangerous course of all,' he said.

The little boy squeezed the wizard's hand tightly, seeking some solace from the old man's strength. 'Am I dreaming?' he asked, still gripping his hand.

'You are here, yet you are somewhere else. There are many places, different spaces that exist simultaneously, like rooms in an endless house. There are lessons to be learned and keys to be acquired, which open these doors. Much of what you learn here you will not be able to remember when you are gone, not straight away. Yet the seed of the memory containing all you need to know is inside you and grows as you do. Together with Athena you must also move your hand. But this you will remember: *Follow the paradoxes* in your mind and they will lead you here. *Innocence is the key* that will open the door, you can only come here as a child. This is why childhood memories are so important, they contain the clues you need to follow to the answers, which are the keys to the places you will have to visit on your path in order to fulfil your purpose in this lifetime. And this here . . .' he said planting his feet in the rock and looking around, '. . . is one of them.'

They were at the top now, looking over the clouds and what looked like the whole world unravelled at their feet. The little boy's eyes were roaming, and he felt as if he was flying.

'To see like an eagle is one thing. To really see through an eagle's eyes, you have to become one!' came the voice of the wizard, and the boy turned to his right to face him, only to stumble backwards, for what he saw was this: his face had turned different colour patches, turquoise, red and white with thick black lines separating them, all glittering like some sand drawing. Instead of hair he had feathers on his head and from his eyes a blue light streaming out. Without a sound he glided on the air, without falling, soaring now, a complete eagle in every shape or form. In the boy's mind he could hear the wizard's voice beckoning 'don't hesitate!' and he took a deep breath, crouching back, loading that spring ready to jump. As he moved forward he seemed to change in mid air, to grow physically as he moved through the air, his body was ageing, becoming that of an adult. He was becoming aware of a strong light in front of him, and realised that it was the Sun.

☯

He could feel his feet pounding the hardened desert soil, lifting clouds of dust into the air. The bright sunlight was blinding him but every time he tried to look away he felt a pain. Something was tugging at him, pulling his flesh on his chest, something like a big bear's claws. The pain was dull, until that tugging feeling, and then it was excruciating and sharp like a jagged blade twisting inside his breasts, tearing at his muscles. He tried to come to his senses, to wake up from what must be a dream but felt it was futile. Slowly however he became conscious of his own movement, as if through a haze and soon realised that the tugging was resulting from his dancing. The sound was the last to come. Through the shuffling sound of his feet on the ground, he started to distinguish a rhythmical beat, from a drum, or drums. Some sort of whistle sound pierced the air far above. His chest was pierced with what looked like two bear's claws attached to a large wooden pole. He started to realise that he was dancing a Sundance. As he became aware of the fact, he turned to look at the other dancers. They were there all right, dancing in a circle around the denuded tree. Their faces looked very familiar to him, brothers from a not so distant past. Looking into the other dancers' eyes he sensed their pain, face contorted, dry lips cracking, teeth gritting on the eagle bone whistle. It was the pained expression on their faces that told the story; it was so unique and personal for each one that he became aware that this was more than a dream involving him only. And if it was a dream at all, the other dancers were there dreaming it with him. The music was intensifying, the Sun blazing onto his skin, burning, his body wild, moving, pulling, pulsating, beckoning, like a wild animal struggling to be free.

All other sounds seemed to drift away, as if a cloud had muffled them, and he heard it again, louder this time, clearer, a piercing sound – an eagle swooping, one step forward now, through the pain, through the fear into the arms of Grandfather Sun. As the piercing sound of the eagle's cry shattered his vision, he jumped back ripping his flesh, from the corners of his eyes barely catching a glimpse of people rushing to catch him as he fell …

He opened his eyes in a blink adjusting to the air gushing past his face. Far below him a valley, water snaking its way down to the hills, at the feet of the mountain, its huge mass a homely presence behind him. He was an eagle. He looked for his arms and saw only wings. He could see great detail over amazing distances, he could feel and even see the wind, he was flying, soaring high above the clouds, where no humans can see. He flew all through the day and into the night, soaring higher and higher above the Earth, until he was amongst the stars themselves.

He heard a distant sound rapidly approaching, but he could see nothing moving towards him.

The distant sound had ceased to be faint or distant. It had become the most amazingly awesome and huge sound, a music coming from the stars and planets themselves like a song. It was almost frightening in magnitude, yet sweet and reassuring, intelligent, primordial and dark, yet full of light, an amazing symphony of sounds, vibrating from each planet and star, every particle of being dancing the dance of creation. Nothing on Earth could come close to this music, but there was something about it which reminded him of the whales' songs.

He felt he was flying in the night over the deep dark ocean. The moon was shining on the waves illuminating an eerie landscape of tall snow peaked jagged mountains. The huge tail of a blue whale disappeared under the surface, leaving but two spiralling eddies as evidence of its presence. Everything started to spin, round and round, images of the wizard, the table, the stars, and the whale.

It all went dark again. Reluctantly he opened his eyes. It was still night time, and he was still in the woods lying in the same spot under the stars. A quick look at the sky confirmed his suspicion that some time had passed, most of the night in fact. Far away he could hear the dull roar of the highway as the early morning traffic started picking up. He got up and stretched his damp body. He hadn't slept, he knew as much, but he wasn't at all tired. His heart felt light, full of joy, for being alive, really alive, that was a blessing and for that he was always grateful. Spiritual experiences like that had happened to him throughout his life, so much that he was less surprised nowadays.

As a child it had all seemed so natural to experience all sorts of things, which to grownups were unreal. The constant denial, belittlement and sarcasm did little to avert his attention, for he knew what he saw, and as he grew older it just meant he had to 'slip away' more discretely, when it was nap time, or when he could hide outdoors under a tree or behind a bush. But as he grew older, there were more and more demands on his time, and less tolerance for 'time wasted' being up in the clouds and 'day dreaming'. His culture didn't have any belief in all that, at least not in any human form, for most priests had long ago lost their faith and become more like privileged civil servants, most of them fat, corrupt and uncaring. The churches retained some of their power, because some people still believe and carry on the real stuff, their hearts leading them to experience some of the symbolic life which becomes the tree out of which comes the wood to make the boat for the spirit journey. So there was something for him to tune in to, in spite of the changing times.

Had he been born in a tribe, life would have been so

much better for him in many ways. He would have had guidance, advice about how to interpret his visions. He would have been taught skills of much more use to him than what western society had to offer. But then again he wouldn't understand this rotten world as well as he does now, and have empathy for those still trapped in the illusions that are endlessly spun around them.

'There's a reason for all this, something of use that will become apparent to me when the time comes, I just have to keep asking the questions, keep my eyes open.' He wandered through the woods headed back towards the city, slowly, reluctantly. He knew, as always, that he had to stay strong now and not let the city bring him down, but instead bring something positive to it from the temple of nature.

CHAPTER 9
THE ISLAND

'I hope you feel better soon. You gotta try not to let this kind of thing incapacitate you though, responsibilities etc, you know,' Mathew was being honest, blunt maybe, but honest. It was difficult getting this on the other end of the line, and Andri just wanted to get off the phone. He called Mathew, at the place they both worked – a residential care home for those with 'mental illness' or so the label goes. He called to say he wasn't going to make it, he was slotted to do the night shift, and he had just last night broken off with his girlfriend Maria, after two very intense years together. He was extremely upset, and couldn't deal with having to be relied upon if anything happened, as it invariably did when you least wanted it to in this home. With six different people living there, and a variety of mental issues, each on a different cycle with a bunch of questionable drugs to keep them 'sane' and well behaved, which sometimes they didn't take to add to the variety of life; it was not a matter of if, but when. And although experience warns you about what is brewing underground, it's as easy to predict when an active volcano will erupt as it is to know when one or more of your 'customers' is going to go off on one.

Anyway, for Andri the pain was physical as well. 'Always fucking incapacitated,' he thought, letting Mathew's words weight him down even more now with the additional issue of responsibility.

'Its early morning, he's got plenty of time to find cover before his shift is over, I don't know what he is complaining about!' he mumbled angrily. He was hurt, and he felt he wasn't handling it well enough. 'Not mature enough, boy is that typical! You feel as deeply as I do, the pain, its intense, really strong like if someone died ... Which is probably why I've had very few serious relationships, it takes me years to get over each one. So many lessons, so much pain, where does it all come from? Am I wrong in letting myself feel this? Should I just ignore it and put on the mask of the 'brave manly man'? I was never one to hide that way, fuck it. There's only one way and that's through it – whatever it takes!' He grinned and folded in half from the pain in his abdomen. The physical pain would subside in a few days hopefully, but the rest ... would take much longer, and much soul searching. You love deep you hurt deep. He knew that was how it worked, and still was happy for the trade-off, it was all worth it. But at times like these it was just the pain that kept him company. It was a warm and sunny Spring day, and somehow that made the break-up even more depressing.

'How easy it would have been,' he though to himself casting his mind back to his first big break-up, after a relationship of seven years that was just as intense in a different way. At that time he had made some important and conscious decisions about his heart. It was at the village where his parents had come from.

☯

His grandma still had an old house there, and he had gone there after the break up to sort himself out. He was so devastated by the break that he had to find retreat and that was a healing place for him, as he came to realise since he was a kid.

This was a place of real people. Their magic was of the heart, their power their living relationship with the Earth, although by now their minds were being invaded by the preoccupations of this age, an endless stream of garbage ranging from politics to sports and fashion. This mental garbage had already proven more destructive to these small communities than the bulldozer of Christianity or the hundreds of years of occupation by the Venetians and later the Ottoman Turks. At least the healing practices and Earth rituals had largely survived by taking on the guise of the new religion, which in turn returned the favour of empowerment by providing asylum to their spirituality during the many years of cultural and religious subjugation.

Nowadays the invasion was more subtle. Tourism was knocking on the door, and although the islanders as a whole had tried to stem the flow and salvage their quality of life the signs were cause for worrying. Andri had looked forward, as always, to a real cup of Greek coffee at the first coffee house by the end of the pier. It gave him that warm feeling of having arrived after the long journey on the ferry, and was necessary to wash away the taste of the dishwater they served on board. He made his way through a cloud of diesel fumes spewing from the heavy trucks, cars and motorcycles. In the summer there would be rows of hotel vans, and crowds of punters offering accommodation but it was still spring and on the pier only a few people waiting for relatives. He made his way to the café, and sat down on a silvery metal chair.

'What happened to the nice traditional wooden chairs you used to have? The ones with the woven seat, much warmer to sit on. Renovation?' he asked in Greek the young waiter who seemed to loom over him as soon as he sat down. The vacuous expression on his face let Andri know that the words had not registered.

'Menu?' the waiter offered politely pulling a shiny and colourful pamphlet and placing it on the table. Andri looked inside. 'Cappuccino, espresso, latte … crepe with apple, berries …' The menu read like something from a big European city café, and to his horror Greek coffee wasn't even on the list!

'What happened to this place then?' he asked in English hoping for some communication.

'Bought it we did, now is much better!' replied the waiter in an impeccable German accent. As he left, Andri took another look to make sure he hadn't walked into another shop. He hadn't.

'Damn it! Have to search for a Greek coffee in Greece!' he thought out loud. Disappointed with the change he left the port and headed to the village.

So there he was in his early 20s, his world literally blown apart from the intensity of emotions, the pain, darkness and despair. People he knew changed relationships like they changed shirts in the morning, but oh no, he had to have the deep feelings, good and bad. So there he stood, praying and in tears, for the pain in his heart to end, when a vision of a breastplate armour like the ones knights wore in the middle ages appeared hovering in front of him in a circle of light. It was a shiny silver colour, suspended in mid-air in front of him as if it was held by some invisible hands. It looked like the one he got from his parents for his fifth birthday, part of a set including a sword and roman helmet. He remembered he hadn't used the helmet then, because he wanted to be a medieval knight and not a roman, but he liked the sword and armour. Something inside was trying to tell him something, he realised that much but what? Had something happened then, when he was a five year old kid, something that hurt him? Quite likely, he always took things at heart and was often hurt by others, although they were more often than not unaware of having hurt him. Maybe the breastplate was just offering protection. Andri realised at that moment that he had a choice, he was standing at the crossroads. He could put on the armour over his heart and never feel any pain again. The breastplate offered him a way out, but it was one that would dull out all his feelings, not just the pain but the joy as well. He realised then how many people subconsciously take the decision to de-sensitize their heart, little by little at so many painful junctions in their lives until they are empty and hollow their true feelings well hidden, their souls imprisoned in a jail of their own making. He was glad for the insight and the clear decision not to put on the armour, a choice which made the pain less strong anyway.

It was still daytime and he decided to go for a walk along the valley towards the springs. The sun was warm, and the light breeze brought the smells of early Spring to his nostrils. It had rained in the night, but the morning sun had already dried out the dirt trail that eventually led to the tiny church of St George, up by the water. The smell of the earth was rich, promising a bountiful harvest for the summer. Beautiful delicate butterflies danced on the smell laden air. All the little creatures were out and about, being busy knowing in their own way that so much depends on them as well.

Andri hadn't met anyone on the way past the village, after all it was a time of day when most of the few inhabitants left would be in the orchards, or otherwise occupied in their homes. He loved them all dearly, but had come here to be mostly on his own. There were exceptions, like his cousin Katerina, with whom he'd climbed up to the church in the cave yesterday. 'Ah, yes, what a magical place!' he said to no one around. He was recalling in his mind the walk through the low thyme and oregano bushes growing everywhere where there were no boulders to cover the soil, and then the approach to the cave itself.

It was a small cave, tall enough to stand in, and deep enough for thirty people or so to squeeze in, very close to the peak of a small mountain on the North side of the village. It looked to the east, facing the mountains in the middle of the island, and just outside the cave was enough space to precariously place a couple of tables, which is what happened once a year when the village gathered there. Many years ago, one of their relatives herding his goats on the slopes had discovered an icon of the nativity inside the cave, and had taken it down to his house. In the night, the icon disappeared, and miraculously appeared back at the cave, as was discovered the next day. And since people listened to the signs of the Spirit in those days, they built a church of the nativity inside the cave. Just inside the entrance, there was a tunnel, going down like a well, which has been blocked after a child had fallen in.

'The story is that the tunnel goes all the way down to the river,' said Andri's cousin, who had been called in her life to take care of the church throughout the year, and was the only person to make regular trips to it. 'You see, back in the middle ages, there was a small monastery down there, more of a retreat, for half a dozen monks or so. You can still see the ruins of the buildings if you walk up that way. Anyway, when the Turks took over the island from the Venetians, the monks moved up to this cave, and barricaded themselves in. As you can see it's too steep to just wander into this place, and it's not even visible from down below, so the Turks didn't find them. But to keep hidden they had to avoid making fires, but they also needed to cook, so at night, one of the monks would climb through the tunnel to the river. On the riverbank a villager would be waiting with provisions, and also a fire which he would have been tending for a while. The monk would take the provisions in a sack, and put some coals in a small metal bucket which he would then take up to the cave for cooking. One evening however, the monk forgot to bring the little bucket. This was risky business to start with, for if anyone saw them there would horrible reprisals on the villagers, and as you have seen the distance is long, so it was out of the question for the monk to go back. "What are you going to do?" asked the villager, knowing that without coal the monks would be hungry. "I'll just have to put the coals on my robe, like this," replied the monk, and proceeded to take the red hot coal in his black cotton robe all the way up to the cave without burning a hole in it. Now that's faith!' she'd said pointing her fingers to the sky.

The narrow path travelled through what was the remnants of the old village, further inland and hidden from the sea by the mountains. Now abandoned for the lack of sea views, it had been well inhabited in the old days, when the threat of pirates and later on the Turks was present. Past the old village Andri soon came upon the ruins of the small monastery he'd seen from the cave. There used to be at least three larger buildings, and a small structure – probably some type of store room. The middle building had been the church, on the North side was the kitchen area, and some kind of workshop, and on the South side the sleeping quarters.

Andri looked around inside sensing the high energy of the place, then walked outside and took some pictures with his camera. He stood on a boulder to get a particular angle shot causing it to roll and ending up on the ground, his elbow taking a knock to protect the camera. His face ended up practically staring at a hollow which had been exposed by the rolling boulder and from the corner of his eye he caught a glimpse of a bone. Cautiously, as he was well aware of the presence of a type of rattlesnake in the area, he stuck his head in. In the hollow he found a neat pile of human bones with a skull on top. He wouldn't normally like to disturb someone's remains, but something inside him moved him to lift the skull. As he touched it a spark of light went through his fingers, like a mild electric shock and he almost lost his balance. 'Careful now!' he cautioned himself. Respectfully he lifted it towards the sun. Without warning he was overcome by a sudden outpouring of feelings, grief. Tears streamed from his eyes, and he knew he was crying for the monk whose skull he held in his palms, but had no idea why. Time seemed to stand still. A butterfly landed gently on his hand for an instance and then fluttered away. A light breeze on his wet face gently brought him back. As if in a dream he placed the skull back and replaced the boulder shoring it up so it wouldn't roll easily. 'What was that all about?' he thought out loud wiping the tears from his eyes. Still dazed he walked back to the trail. He though he heard the characteristic splashing sound of the sea against the cheek of a sailing boat's hull, but the coast was miles away and the wind was blowing away from the shore. He steadied himself and fumbled in his pocket for his rolling tobacco.

'Why me?' he asked facing the sun. He thought of all those really suffering on this planet, the war, hunger and homelessness so many have to endure daily, as he often did when he caught himself complaining about his lot. 'Ok, you're right, I should be thankful, I am thankful,' he murmured.

CHAPTER 10
THE MONK'S STORY

The summer sun was blazing unobstructed onto the dry dirt road. Barely held back by the well travelled rocky cut in the landscape Mother Nature was going wild, with green trees and bushes covering every available space as if they knew this was sacred ground, a great place to grow. Gregory was in his twenties, lean and tall with short brown hair and a face that was well acquainted with the sun's rays. He was wearing a well worn monk's robe that didn't quite fit him, and sandals that had seen too many miles. To find 'the truth' about life was what his quest had been for a few years now, and this peninsula in Northern Greece his latest adventure. Almost anxious to get there, and with the wings of youth on his ankles, he rushed along nearly running into a figure wearing a heavy black robe, hood on the head.

'I do apologise!' he exclaimed, 'are you all right?'

'Yes, thank you,' replied the monk. 'What's your rush? We're all going to die some day! Take my advice young man, walk slowly and you won't sweat, that way you can go farther,' he added with a father to son tone. Gregory thanked him for his advice and asked him if there were any knowledgeable healers in the area. As the pair walked together they found themselves crossing into the grounds of a monastery's orchard, full of fruit trees, apples, pears, oranges and lemons.

'The monastery is just around the next bend,' said the monk, and soon enough it came into view. It looked more like a castle on the edge of the sea, heavily fortified to keep out all sorts of marauding pirates and even 'regular' armies, such as the crusaders. Now the Ottoman Turks was the main concern. Although they taxed the monasteries heavily, they pretty much left the monks to their own devices, but travelling there was still a dangerous affair.

'As for the healing arts a good place to start is there,' he replied pointing to a monk sitting on a wooden bench on the approach to the monastery's heavy studded oak gates. 'We found him wandering about in the woods a year ago now, and it seems he was in there for a few months on his own – he doesn't remember much of that apart from some experiences of light. He won't talk about it, and no-one is sure if he remembers anything at all, but he gives me the feeling he's been to hell and back. Who knows, a former soldier perhaps. One thing's for certain, he knows something about healing . . . I'm going off this way, tending the goats' needs now,' he said raising his hand. Gregory reciprocated the gesture and headed towards the monastery.

'Don't talk to him, he's crazy!' shouted the monk jokingly from a distance.

'Well, they say that only from a child or a fool you will

find the truth, so here goes,' thought Gregory to himself. The old monk beckoned him to sit next to him on the old wooden bench. The grapevines weaved into the trellis above them provided a much needed shade, for not only was it August, but the middle of the day as well and there was not a cloud in the sky – apart from on the top of the holy mountain itself.

The peak there was always covered by clouds, even when there was not one other cloud in the whole sky. On the icons there was always an image of the Theotokos Maria in the midst of those clouds overlooking the many monasteries. No females were allowed in the whole peninsula where the monasteries had been built, not even female animals. Gregory, who was a scholar of the esoteric traditions was well aware that the monks revered the Theotokos above all, and that She acted as a temple for them to heal their experiences with women in their lives. As the Earth Mother She also sanctified their healing practices, many of which were still very pagan in origin. It was his interest in this area of healing that brought him to this monastery, and the rumours of some real miracles happening in this area. Gregory looked at the old monk's face, calm green eyes amidst wrinkles like deep furrows indicating a past of intense emotions, joy and pain. He couldn't make up his mind about which was prevalent when a slight change in the old man's eyes gave him the clear answer. This man had suffered untold situations.

'I won't waste your time ...' Gregory started and then stopped realising the monk had already decided to talk to him and instead of wasting his time he ought to get on with it.

He couldn't decide what to ask him first, about the search for the truth, or about healing practices, when the old man spoke.

'I was young once and searching, just like you. I too was travelling to wherever I heard of as a happening place, gathering my little experiences in this old sack,' he said pinching the skin on his left arm, 'looking for the magic that would shake the world, and clean it from all this disease and suffering.'

'And what did you find old man?' asked Gregory hoping for some sort of short and amazing answer, expecting a mundane standard church doctrine answer instead.

'For me it comes back to a story about a monk, a pirate and a witch behind bars, in a cage on a horse drawn cart, paraded through the town of Naxos in Sicily,' said the monk. 'No human ears have ever heard this story before, and I will tell it only once, so listen carefully to the details.' The quality of his voice had changed, and the heat was shifting the moisture from the ground making everything hazy. A story was as good an answer as any, and it certainly sounded interesting enough. Gregory took a sip from his flask and handed it to the monk who politely declined, saying he would just sweat it out anyway. The sea was only a couple hundred meters from where they were seated, and the gentle lapping of the waves on the granite rocks by the base of the monastery of Stavronikita made his eyelids heavy. He closed his eyes and listened, being gently carried away into the old monk's story.

‘The hull of the boat was smashing against the waves making a deafening sound. The 77 foot wooden sail boat was strong enough to take the lashing of the smaller waves, getting bigger now they were approaching the edge of the rocky island just outside the cape, where the open sea ahead of them was raging.

Most people would quickly classify the motley crew as ‘pirates’, and that was no mean achievement in these confusing times. Now that the fourth crusade was almost over, there were quite a few of difficult to classify ‘organised freelancers’ of the seas one could say. Most of them were a more or less known façade for some influential interest group, allied to some part of the Mediterranean, and to some religious group. From the Knights of St. John, the Hospitalliers, who targeted mainly Turkish cargo ships – to Aruj Barbarossa himself, who targeted anything but especially the Christian ships the whole spectrum of economic interests was represented by some form of ‘pirate outfit’. However, for most people Captain Death, as he liked to be known by his enemies, ‘which includes just about anyone whom I don’t know, so they might as well be afraid of me! Har!’ he shouted, banging his fist on the heavy oak table and making everything on it jump, and then burst laughing, as did everyone else, for they knew that he really was a sweet, kind and life loving person. Tall and thin, but strong and full of muscle, his jet black hair and beard gave him a sombre and menacing appearance. This he liked to accentuate by tying red strips of cloth on his clothes with small bones attached on the ends. They were actually animal bones, worn for his protection, but to all else the effect was more like death. For his friends he was just Captain or John, someone they could depend upon to protect the community from all he called the 'true' pirates, for their game is destruction, death and disease. And yet, in the eyes of most 'decent' law abiding citizens John and his crew were the worst kind of pirates, and most feared. So the crew would take *the Blade* as the boat was named, again to use the edge of the mind rather than the sword, and attack the ports and the ships around them, spread some decent terror to last until the next time, stock up with provisions and off to the hidden island community.

This was going to be another one of those expeditions, as the community was running low of essential supplies, and the armed escort and other 'military' ships seemed to be on the move away from that part of the sea – close to Sicily. It was a bit risky, they all knew that from the start, because the season wasn't right for such large scale activities, and according to their intelligence from the mainland, the big towns of Genoa and Venice, nothing was brewing warwise to justify it. There was instead the dangerous rumour of a trap being set, to capture them. Yet the remote island was a secluded place, and the long winter was going to add to the population; with a few women already pregnant the needs of the community were becoming more pressing.

'We have no choice but to go and hope for the best,' said John to the crew as they sat in the warm room. The fire was cracking, and the 'Only pub in town' as they had jokingly baptised the place was packed, as every evening as it doubled as the 'only kitchen in town' for communal feeding.

‘For one thing we need more food and supplies. But most importantly we need more spirits!’ his laughter was instantly contagious as everyone felt the danger lying ahead. Now, they knew why they had those feelings all along.

‘They were planning this for months, the pigs!’ shouted Nicolas to overcome the roar of the wind. ‘They can’t have it, it drives them crazy that we’ve escaped their claws for so many years, and flouted our freedom!’ Nicolas was John’s right hand man, even taller than John and built like a bull. He wasn’t one to shy from a fight, but the sudden appearance of a dozen well armed galley ships at the southern mouth of the cape was an alarming sight for anyone, let alone the most wanted pirate of the area. The bigger and harder to manoeuvre galleys would normally be easy for *the Blade* to outrun, a two mast Brigantine with oars powered by a free crew and not slaves. But this time the Spanish and Venetian ships were prepared, sailing just out of sight with all sails out and ready to pounce.

‘Maybe we did a bit too much of that and showed them something we shouldn’t have …’ reflected John. ‘All hands to the oars!’ he commanded.

‘Or a spy! How else would they know?’ asked Nicolas obviously agitated by his friend’s refusal to look at the obvious – almost naïve how he always looked for the good in people.

‘All possibilities will need to be explored, but for now we have a good run ahead of us to shake them off. If we can’t outrun them, and it seems we can’t, they were to close and caught us by surprise, well have to head for the storm and sink them.’ John had a stern look on his face, one that contemplated unpalatable outcomes.

'If this is indeed a betrayal, we better make haste for the island. The community might be under attack,' said Nicolas, who had come next to John both holding on the railing close to the steering wheel.

'It might be so,' said John. 'But also, it might be a bait, to make us lead them there. Just in case, we aught to be cautious and make sure we give them the slip before we head for the island,' he said. Nicolas nodded, but his gut was uncomfortable, a sense of urgency unsettling him. They were headed straight for the storm, so things would soon start shaking. It was time for the ropes and the circle.

Most of the crew were already on deck, securing the foresail and main sails and anything else that could drag them in the sea if they made a wrong move on the high waves. It was time for the centring and the calling of the powers of the sea and the air, the fire within and the earth below.

The first time they did the circle in the high seas they all questioned Esmeralda's vision, and there was quite a struggle between John and the crew. It had been especially difficult for him to convince them all that it could work, let alone that it would work, because she was also his lover. The women in the community were more eager to try it out than the men, since theirs was a central role in the vision, although Esmeralda was an outsider to the community, and didn't live there permanently but rather was one of the few people allowed to visit. 'I can do much more from the outside,' she insisted at that meeting, 'and if you don't trust me then pull your blade now and finish it!' she shouted. Nicolas wasn't about to use a blade on a woman, let alone his friend's love – for John did love her, so much was obvious from the start. It was in fact the strength of that relationship, which convinced him to agree with such a dangerous experiment. Esmeralda was a witch, he knew that much from her healing practices, some of which he had witnessed himself. But this vision was something else, and the only way to find out if it was a divine message was to try it out, in the storm. And so surprised they were when it worked, that she became something of a priestess for the community ever since.

The twelve 'navigators' were assembled around the main mast. Four maidens in the middle holding hands in a circle, marking the four elements Earth, Wind, Fire and Water. Around them, in a second circle, another eight people, four men and four women. The time for the stillness had arrived.

They had just cleared the rocks at the edge of the land and were swiftly making their way towards the open sea and the raging storm. The waves already twenty foot high under a dark foreboding sky were twisting the old boat making every joint scrape and scream whilst the wood groaned.

'Keep her steady, we're going in!' shouted John to the crew who were dancing around the deck getting themselves lashed to the rails by their posts. Soon all was ready. The enemy ships had split up, most falling back to the safety of the harbour, with only a handful now continuing pursuit. John and Nicolas looked at each other and onto the deck. The scene there was so alien to what the eye expects that it never ceased to amaze them both. Surrounding the boat was water, in huge dark waves, with just a corner of the sky visible. The boat had been going up and down the enormous mountains of water with only a tiny triangle sail open – the flying jib- to keep the stern pressed in so it could be steered. On the main deck, the circle of four women, who seemed to have grown in stature, their colourful robes and long hair lifted by the wind like feathers on a soaring eagle. Surrounding them the second circle, dancing around them and chanting something mysterious. It all looked like it belonged somewhere in the deep woods, but not on a deck of a ship, in a storm! The sky had turned black and thundering, rain coming down as if the sea had emptied and needed replenishing. There was no sight of the other ships now, wouldn't be able to see them even at 50 yards in this storm anyway.

The chanting was starting to intensify. In the utter darkness of the storm the lightning gave an eerie interrupted view of the liquid landscape.

'AAAAAAAAAUUUUUUMMMMMMMM'

A shimmering golden light appeared at the edge of the outer circle and started getting brighter and brighter covering the dancers and the priestesses in what looked like a round turtle shell. From the centre of it a thin ray of blue light beamed towards the heavens. The *Blade* was by now at the eye of the storm, and all seemed to have quietened down. The eerie silence was pushed aside by a gentle humming sound, like a huge swarm of bees growing by the second, until the air crackled and the ship was drenched in a pillar of light in what seemed like an explosion of colours. Most of the crew had similar experiences of what followed. John had expressed it well for all when he described it as, '. . . a feeling of being lifted up in the sky by a huge eagle who is carrying the sun in his talons,' and invariably when they came to from what seemed like a deep sleep they always found themselves on the other side of the storm, having eluded their suitors. It was generally believed that people weren't meant to see these beings, and they'd go mad if they did, but some suspected that John remembered more than that, because he was always the first one to wake up, or even that he stayed awake through it, but he wouldn't say a word more about it. Whatever the deal was between the crew of the *Blade* and the powers that made their free community viable was surely a secret entrusted only to him.

'If we needed to know, we would. Its safer this way, that's what he told me, and if there was anything to tell anyone he would certainly tell me first,' Nicolas had said to the rest of the crew when the issue had come up after the roundup meeting, as they called their self administration court. After all the community had no leader, and that was the deal. But they all agreed to a captain for the ship, and the idea of someone who acted in the group's interest soon found bones in John.

Nicolas slowly opened his eyes and looked around. He was surprised to see that John was still coming to, and not waking him up as was usually the case. John was obviously shocked at the realisation of that when he managed to focus on Nicolas and jumped up holding his chest as if there was something missing there.

'What is it?' asked Nicolas, disconcerted by his friend's reaction.

'I'm not sure, but something is terribly wrong, I can feel

it,' replied John in a whisper. 'I feel like I've been kicked in the chest by a mule,' he said more loudly, standing himself up and looking now to see where they had ended up.

'Close to Sicily, by the village Esmeralda lives' said Nicolas as if reading his mind. 'We should turn around and head for the island, anyway she could well be there, and we've got to make sure everything's all right before we venture anywhere again,' said Nicolas, implying the traitor had to be found.

'All right,' said John reluctantly. He knew he had to put the welfare of the community first, but his senses told him they were all right and yet undetected. But what had happened in the storm troubled him. This time they hadn't allowed him to stay awake. For the first time he too had lost consciousness during the trip. There was something they didn't want him to know, or at least not yet, and that left him blind, directionless. Apart from Esme, he had to see her and soon. His mind wandered back to the first time he saw her. It was in her garden, a typical witch's patch full of strange and common healing herbs that will cure almost anything, provided you knew how to tend them and prepare them. He was carrying a wounded friend, another pirate, back in the days they had a small boat and crew of a handful or two. Out to get the small freighters, or raid an isolated settlement they barely scraped a living, hardly worth the risk. On that particular occasion they had encountered an armed Venetian escort ship, or rather been encountered by it in the dark. The resultant fight was brief, more of a hasty getaway, but had left one of them injured. He was in a bad way and had to be patched up if he was to have a chance. Some folk up the coast there gave them directions to the witch's hut. She had surprised them both by creeping on them from behind.

'What do you want?' she had asked. 'Help, for my wounded companion here,' he'd replied. 'And what makes you think I would, that is to say if I even could, help a bleeding pirate?' she'd asked moving into clear view. She looked at him from a place of power, and he immediately sensed it. She was in her twenties, of average height, long brown red curly hair waving past her shoulders. Her eyes were like the sky on a clear day, warm but strong and fiery. She appeared thin, but also gave the impression of a well exercised body. John had gone entirely silent. 'Oh, don't just stand there then like an idiot, bring him inside,' she had said. The days of the healing he helped her with the firewood, fetching water, and preparing the herbs. When his friend was well enough to leave, he had stood there in the garden with her, looking for words to express what he hadn't known before and could not describe. She'd put her fingers on his lips and stared through his eyes it seemed and into his soul.

'You can't help me, leave and never come back,' she warned, but he couldn't listen. His heart was melting and burning through his guts. She stepped back. She had a lot to be thankful for, the healing had gone well, and once again she felt she was in tune with the Spirit, after a long period of drought. She'd lost her faith when, in spite of years of training, she found herself incapable of helping her mother in her final illness. It took her a long time to accept what her mother had warned her about, accepting the price that she could not heal her own lineage. 'An odd pact with the Spirit' her mother had called it, 'to make sure we don't forget how small we are in the scheme of things, so we make the right choices in life. It's a gift in disguise really, better now than later, all at the end is too much pain to deal with,' she'd said, although Esme never understood why she said that bit about later, as she died soon after that and as a witch she was well aware of her approaching passage.

He wrapped his right arm around her bare waist and drew her closer. He could feel the tiny hairs on her skin rise as he brought her navel close to his. His left hand gently caressed her shoulder, then her neck, catching a drop of sweat by her collar bone. Their lips quivered, then touched. They kissed for an eternity, and then kissed again. The world was never the same for either of them. A door had been thrown open asunder, and nothing could ever close it again.

After the community had developed and they moved to the island, he'd realised that it could be no coincidence he met her, that no other could have been there to help them like she did. In the old days she would have been a priestess, a wise woman, revered and safe in her power. Nowadays she was a witch, hiding from the church and its cronies but still harboured by the rural communities, as she is their only healer, now that the official religion has denounced all that. And although at risk, she wouldn't leave the villages where she grew up to go to the island.

'Why don't you become a farmer then,' she'd said to him when he asked her to move out there. He knew he could not turn her mind when it was set, so reluctantly had agreed to occasional visits instead.

'Almost there now, I can see the smoke from the village,'

said Nicolas, tearing John away from his thoughts.

'You shouldn't be able to see the smoke from this far,' replied John, making for the stern of *the Blade*.

As the ship cleared the rocky North side of the small island, the wreck of a Venetian ship appeared in front of them.

'Thank God for the reefs!' exclaimed Nicolas. 'No sign of the crew though, must have made it ashore,' he added. Their worries were soon dispersed, when the village came to view, and they realised the source of the fire was a floating part of the wreck which was ablaze and not the houses of the settlement. Soon all was confirmed by the crowd gathered on the beach, brandishing the shields and swords of their dead enemies with pride, especially the young ones who were the majority of the population when the ship was on a mission, most dads and moms being on board.

☯

The reunion was full of tears of relief and tales of bravery as they all made for the tavern. Soon inside the gathered crew were listening to Crawley, who was too old to be on deck but more than happy to run the cellar of the tavern, laying it out. The ship was alone, but obviously looking for them. It sank by the entrance of the harbour, and the crew that survived were killed in the 'epic battle, of which I took a leading role,' said Crawley, interrupted by some lads from the back shouting 'yeah, straight to the cellar!' and everyone burst out laughing while Crawley was left stuttering about how he had to save the supplies and all! A few moments later he took John and Nicolas by the side.

'There's a spy,' he said in a low whisper. 'I suspected as much!' replied Nicolas.

'We questioned one of the crew before he passed on, and he told us there are boats headed to Sicily, "to rat out the damn witch" he said. You've got little time if that!' Crawley was a decent man, and although his wife had died when they were young, he never took another partner. He was praying inside and would continue to pray for Esmeralda's safety. 'May the Spirit help you!' he said when parting. 'May it help us all,' replied Nicolas. John was already on his way to the find a few volunteers for a desperate rescue mission.

John was using all he knew and more he was discovering on the way, to get *the Blade* moving. Considering there was little wind to start with, they were doing well. The wind had picked up considerably as the small crew danced around the deck adjusting the sails to get the best of them they could. He had focused on summoning the winds to take them there, and it seemed that someone was listening, the South-westerly was rare this time of year but had made a special appearance for the occasion. It was cloudy and he couldn't tell what time of day it was, but his internal clock told him it was near dusk. The wind picked up as the sky darkened, accompanied by occasional sleet and rain. He'd left Nicolas on the wheel and moved to the bow, holding on to the front mast. The spray from *the Blade* cutting the waves was forming a thin watery curtain around him. Somehow suddenly he felt all alone. He kept remembering things about her, as if it was happening right in front of him, as if he was just a spectator.

‘Do you realise what’s happening to us?’ she said.

He looked at her marvelling at her beauty, her delicate features hiding her real toughness. He knew somehow that she had been through a lot, most of which she never talked about. He could tell she had wounds in her soul, and a fate with deep roots. This he knew at some level because he was like that himself, and was starting to recognise this. Even the little things she did, the way she touched the leaves of a plant, the care she took of the small creatures, even the stones in her garden it all revealed a person with a strong heart, and one that had been laid to the service of others at her own life’s risk.

‘Can I interrupt your day dream please?’ she said in a more insistent tone, letting you know she was about to say something serious.

‘All right,’ replied John, ‘... so long I can still hold you.’ Making a move towards her.

‘Now stop that!’ she giggled moving her arms up and around. ‘I want to talk. One day we might not have the time, so I want to tell you something important.’ Her voice was strong but could not hide the sadness. John moved his hand to caress her face, but she took it firmly in hers and placed it on her chest. She held it there gently.

‘You know how I feel about you. You are just as precious to me as life itself. For what I do, the healing and magic, it is my role, what I was brought up for and trained all my life. It’s a calling and the powers that work through me are what does the healing, I just make the invitation. But you, what we have shared together, that’s for me, for my soul. You are my medicine and I am yours.' She paused and looked at him in the eyes trying to find the right words and the strength to utter them. He always seemed to have that effect on her, of sending her off to inner spaces, where visions often wandered in. Like when she first met him, and tried to warn him off. The moments before that she had seen her own death and it wasn't pretty. But these past couple of years, with him on her side she kept on fighting it, trying to change it. And then lately something had changed, as if they crossed a threshold together, and she sensed a new life for her and him.

'It's the alchemy. It can change things, and for us I think it has. It's not as simple when a witch and a wizard get together. Oh yes, I know you see the warrior side of yourself, that one is obvious, but behind that you can bring about some powerful energies together. And that is definitely the domain of wizardry. So something magical is happening, to us. I know that, I can feel it in my guts, so I wanted you to know, its all going to be fine ...'

☯

It had been a couple of months since then, and he hardly had the chance to see her with all that was going on. His friends in Venice it seems were onto something big, and he had taken the trip to give them a hand. 'A week, two at most!' he'd promised her when he left, not knowing how deeply involved he would get with that lot, and all those new and exciting possibilities! It seemed then like a real revolution was afoot, now it all seemed dark and uncertain. He wished now he'd told her then how he felt. She knew, certainly, but not quite. He wished he could tell her how deeply he felt for her. How she transformed his life by giving him the most valuable of gifts, that inner knowledge that God loves each and every one of us. How he too had already committed his life to the service of that Divine Love, just like her, and that his biggest struggle was to be unselfish, for more than anything he wanted to spend time with her and grow old with her in his arms. He hadn't been a loner before, and had two children amongst those in the community which came from his seed, but since meeting her he couldn't even think of himself with someone else. She was the light he found on the path, and she lit the whole forest for him. He wanted to tell her how he could feel her soul so close to his that if he was an eagle's wing, she would be the other, with nothing but the heart of the Spirit hovering above the Earth between them.

'Land ahoy!' He heard the mate's voice as if it was coming from another world. Sicily was starting to become visible somewhere in the distant haze. In front of him he could make out the distant shores and their usual anchorage in the hidden bay behind the village.

☯

Esmeralda had her eyes wide open, but was looking only inside. She was remembering how witches are supposed to have a last glimpse of the distant future, a prophetic vision of their own lineage, just before they die, and what her mother had told her at her deathbed.

'I'm sorry Esme, I wish I could have taken some of your burden off for you, but the Spirit tells me it's because you're stronger, you can deal with it and carry it through. It's a blessing I could do without, oh how I wish I wasn't what I am!' She'd told her mother off for speaking that way, as if she was going to die, although she knew she was. But now, she knew why her mother had said that, and that she had meant it. A tear rolled off her cheek, and she felt her tummy with her hand, the baby stirring inside. She looked through the bars of the cage as the cart that was carrying them up the hill to the burning place creaked under the heavy load on the bumpy cobble stone path wending its way through the village. The village where she had worked so much healing, people peering from behind wooden shutters – afraid, others, mostly kids, shouting at her and throwing stones whilst the soldiers, led by the captain of the Sant' Ufficio himself still holding in his hands her Book of Shadows – evidence enough to convict her, surrounded the dark procession, always on the lookout for him. She was hoping he would save her, but she knew he couldn't and was praying to the Spirit to keep him away, out of harm's way. Then she saw him, bursting through the trees – a glimpse, she pointed to her hand resting on her exposed tummy, and then he disappeared.

She pulled her focus back inside, towards the baby, barely noticing the crowds, mothers and children also joining in with the weird procession, a mix of fear, hatred and love. Oh yes, there was some out there for her, she could feel it, someone she healed, someone she touched somehow ... She sank deeper inside, focusing, gathering her strength, praying ... The soldiers were finished tying her to the stake, it wouldn't be long now ... Right there, focusing right on the link with her daughter, she had known it was a girl right from the start ... She could feel the heat and the noise from the crowd roaring together, keep praying ....

A gunshot ripped through the air, a bullet right through her heart.

She was caught by surprise, still, she had been praying to take the child with her, she knew it would otherwise last a bit longer than her, and that she had but one chance, one moment before they were separated to go down their own death birthing channel, one moment to embrace her, to give her the love for a lifetime all at once, and this moment she knew she had already been granted.

Their hands touched, and as they embraced for the first and last time, they were engulfed by a warm golden sphere of light.

A lifetime in one moment.

The crowds slowly dispersed, a mother dragging her child along, 'Come on now, it's over, I think the heat's gone to your head,' she said, her little child insisting that she'd seen a bright light in the fire, 'it was Mary and Jesus, only Jesus was a girl!'

☯

The water was lapping on the side of the boat as it drifted slowly in the open sea. They'd left the coast on a strong wind, but now it had subsided to a light breeze which kept them moving but at a slow clip. 'He's coming to' said Francisco, the Spanish cook who like all of them was also a good warrior.

'Well, I hope I don't have to bash him over the head

again,' said Nicolas, looking on at John's body, which was starting to stir. He wondered if they had actually tied him to the mast or not. It was all a blur. When John jumped out of the woods he knew he had to act fast, and that he wasn't going to be thanked for it later. He'd bashed him on the head and quickly dragged him away to safety. After all he had promised her to keep John safe, she must have known something was due to happen to her, she always seemed to know. And yet she went on with it, accepting it. He had the most respect for her, and John was his best friend, so although it will always haunt him, he did use the rifle. One shot in the heart. He waited until the fire was roaring around her, to make sure there was no chance of saving her. He didn't miss.

John was standing up, pulling desperately at the ropes binding him to the mast, roaring like a wounded bear. Every now and then he'd fall on his knees exhausted and crying uncontrollably, and then he'd lash out and try to free himself, screaming in agonising pain. It was hard to watch their own friend in such pain, as the ropes were turning red from John's blood, but they all knew that if he wasn't tied up he would be straight in the sea, even if Sicily was miles away by now, even if the inquisition and the soldiers from Spain had long gone, even if she was already burnt to ashes. There had been no time for a second shot, as the soldiers were expecting them to show up and were ready, explained Nicolas, even if they had known she was carrying a baby. At least they didn't let the bastards burn her alive. Nicolas collapsed on his knees holding his head between his hands and started crying.

From the soles of your feet to the top of your head – your body is the gate to the garden of your soul, which drinks from the healing waters, from the spring that flows through the stone and pours out inside a cave deep in the Earth. And on the still water a candle is floating, burning with the eternal flame.

CHAPTER 11

THE MOUNTAIN

Gregory sat in stunned silence for a few minutes. He wiped the one tear that got away and cleared his throat.

'How did he survive such a blow?' he asked finally with a new found tenderness. The old monk raised his eyes from the sea to the sky. The air around him seemed to change like an orchestra preparing to play another piece. The breeze caressed the wild flowers who gave it fresh scents to carry around. A passing sparrow voiced its approval with a happy chirp fluttering and swaying above their heads and then it was gone.

'It was the pipe in the end, Guisepe had seen it right.' The voice of the old monk had caught the empty moment like a sail catches the rising wind. 'After they reached the island his mates kept John tied up in fear of what he might do. They had to let him go at the end when he refused to drink or eat anything threatening starvation. In the meantime news came that his friends in Venice had been wiped out, massacred whilst they danced around a fire and the community was in disarray, suspicion and fear tearing it at the seams. He left the island immediately after, on a small sailboat and drifted aimlessly for days, weeks. At the end he landed on the mainland somewhere close to Genoa, and headed North, towards the tall mountains, eating from the land only rats and mice, feeling unworthy of food another human could eat. He carried with him only his dagger, his sabre and a leather bag with the pipe and some flints.

John had been a pirate all his life and what made him so strong in battle was his fearlessness. He had a little secret he'd told no one, not even Esme. He knew he wasn't going to die at sea. He'd seen his death, on top of a tall mountain, alone. Now he wanted to end it, so he followed his vision to the North, past Genoa and Milan and into the tall mountains.

The Summer had long gone, and the cool northern winds were gathering and preparing for their season of action. The first messengers of Autumn had swept through the region during the last moon and the turning leaves were now signalling their readiness. John was walking through the foothills, a couple of days walk past the big lakes. The gently ascending path snaked through the increasingly dense forest, the oak, beech and maple giving way to the tall pines. Large swaths of birch outlined the creeks and ponds. The heavy smell of decaying leaves and moist rich soil was gradually overtaken by the lighter cleansing essence of the pine needles. Straight up through the tall trees John could see the dark rain clouds parading in front of the Sun. A heavy animal scent cut through the forest air and lingered above the wide trail. John's well honed senses quickly deciphered the origin. Human animals. He looked carefully at the ground. Further up he found what he was looking for. The cart wheel tracks were now visible by the side of the trail on the softer ground. Following the pattern of his journey, he took the evasive route through the thick brush. Animals he didn't mind, they seemed to like to keep him company on this trip, perhaps they could sense he would not return. But people, they were the worst animals of all, greedy, selfish, ready to destroy anything good and pure. He circled around the cart. It was easy to spot, a noisy bunch including some children. He moved in closer to take a look before he moved on. A middle aged man, balding and overweight was struggling by the side of a narrow, canvas covered cart. It looked well stuck in the mud where a small creek crossed the trail. Around him three children were playing. Two girls, the eldest no older than ten years old were skipping along and gathering flowers. By the creek a little boy about half that age was filling a flask with water. John remembered the children on the island he left behind. He couldn't help them any more, but he could help these kids. In spite of his weeks of isolation he decided to step out into the open.

'Hi there. Looks like you need some help. I'm not a bandit. I can help if you like.' He shouted from a safe distance. The man jumped back clumsily almost losing his balance. The sight of the old pirate who had been living like a wild animal for a few weeks was enough to scare a young knight, let alone himself. However the stranger could have easily snuck up on them if he meant harm, and by himself he was truly stuck. He gathered his courage and shouted back.

'Yes, please do. We would all be very grateful.'

John approached the cart slowly, giving them enough time to see that he wasn't armed. He stashed his weapons by the path before he walked out into the open. 'The cart looks heavy, maybe we should unload it first,' he commented.

'Can't do it,' replied the man, 'my younger brother is in there, and he is too ill to move. We've taken him all the way to the city to the surgeons, but they said they couldn't do anything for him, so we are going back home, nothing else we can do.' The man lifted the flap at the back of the cart revealing a man so thin he looked dead already. He stirred to move his face away from the sudden intrusion of sunlight onto his grey skin. The flap closed.

'As you can see . . .' the man bowed his head and sighed.

'What about the children, their mother?' enquired John. The kids were all behind their father, tugging on his trousers and peeking from behind at the wild stranger. 'Go on kids, see if you can find some mushrooms over there.' The father motioned towards a small clearing made by a large fallen pine as the children scattered giggling. 'Their mother passed away four years ago, died after giving birth to my son. Couldn't stop the bleeding, the midwife said she had a weak disposition. A couple of years later my brother fell ill and has been getting worse ever since. So it's down to me for now, the children help as they can but they're still too young for the farm work.' He looked at John inquisitively but rightly sensed that he wasn't going to talk about himself.

'And your brother? Does he have any other family?' John had found a strong thick branch and stuck it under the cart wheel levering it up with a boulder.

'No, he never married, never met anyone he was that interested in I suppose. I needed a family, to run the farm, so I married. She was a good woman and we kept each other company. But my brother, well he was a loner really, not very good with people. Brilliant with animals though, always knew what to do for them, and he had good hands for working the leather, made some beautiful things in his day. Too good for this world though, too pure ...'

Setting their shoulders on the back corners of the cart frame they pushed together. Although overweight, the man could push well being accustomed to the hard work of a hillside holding and soon the cart was back on the sturdy part of the trail.

They walked together in silence for a mile or so to the farm, where the farmer invited him in for some food. John declined politely and started to leave. There was some commotion amongst the children and at the end the older girl who was being pushed by her younger siblings, stepped up to him and offered him a chain of tiny white and yellow flowers they had made for him to thank him for his help. He smiled at her and gently took the flower chain and placed it in his bag. Turning towards the trail he realised he hadn't smiled since that day.

'Oh Esme,' he whispered to the trees. The sun was setting behind the dark clouds and a soft rain spread droplets of water on the green canopy, trickling off the fire yellow- red leaves and the pine needles clusters onto his already tear soaked face.

Another mile or so along the path he set up a couple of snares and made a small fire for the night. He was tired for the first time in weeks and slept a deep dreamless sleep. In the morning he walked back to the farm with a hare he'd snared and left it by the door making sure he wasn't seen.

The trail led on and a couple of days later he was leaving the hills behind, and entering the deep mountain valleys. The weather had turned and it was raining on and off. The rivers were swelling from the hard rain forcing him on the higher mountain paths. The steep razor edge mountains further up north were always covered in deep snow, but here in the south of the range he could still get up to the peaks. He picked the one mountain he knew so well, the one where he climbed with Guisepe, the one with the bear cave he never found. He made his last camp before the steep rocky ascent.

In the middle of the night he woke up startled. The image of a woman's hand touching his arm as if to wake him up came to him as an edge of a dream, a tiny corner of a page from a big book ripped off now. Her skin was smooth although she wasn't young, a shiny silver colour. It wasn't Esme, her hands were as tough as they were gentle, her skin almost olive in colour. He sat up and looked around. The clearing he chose in the dark seemed familiar now in the starlight. The clouds had gone for now and there was an almost eerie stillness about the place. He could hear no animals skittering in the undergrowth, no night birds fluttering, no insects buzzing, nothing. Yet there was movement, he wasn't alone. Somewhere behind the trees beyond the clearing he noticed a faint light moving. Then another, and another ...

'Spirits of the woods!' he exclaimed to himself. He remembered now why the clearing seemed familiar to him, it was the same spot they'd encountered the spirits on the trip with Guisepe. Just like then he found he couldn't move, an invisible force seemed to pin him down whilst the spirits danced around him. And then suddenly they were gone. His body slumped backwards from its own weight, released. He thought about Guisepe. The words were still floating about in his head, when he overheard Nicolas talking about the circle in Venice and how they were betrayed and slaughtered by the ancient temple, but he couldn't put it all together yet. Somewhere in there he knew that Guisepe was dead, but he couldn't understand it, any of it. Just when he needed him the most ...

The next day the sun rose behind the dark clouds, which stacked themselves up as far as they could to keep the light away. It was cold and felt like snow was on its way. A freezing drizzle was being blow on the rock face by a spiralling gusty wind, making the rocks slippery. John had buried his sabre in the woods, but he kept the dagger for the climb. The strong sharp blade was easy to wedge between the rocks and although it was taking a beating it only had to last for this one climb. He was halfway up the rock face when he found a ledge which seemed to wrap around the mountain. He sheltered there for a while to warm his fingers, by now almost frozen stiff. If he wanted to go all the way up he had to regain his grip. The thought of ending it there by jumping off the ledge occurred to him. 'No, I'll do it the way I saw it, on the peak,' he decided. The ledge, although narrow where he sat, seemed to widen further along, and he remembered that Guisepe had described such a place when he talked about the bear cave. That was all in the past now he told himself and soon was on his way up the final ascent. Towards the end he had to grit his teeth and muster all his remaining strength pulling at the bottom of his reserves to regain feeling in his right hand and pull his body up to the peak. He growled involuntarily, a terrifying deep sound like a big bear.

The peak was bare and jagged, sharp limestone outcrops reaching for the sky. The wind was fast and furious, blowing ice crystals with force on his face. He scrambled for the base of a couple of big boulders to keep from being blown off. There he was, ready to die yet looking for shelter from the wind, how ironic he thought. At last he found it, a space between the rocks a couple of yards wide, where the howling wind was kept a bay. He settled in propping his back up on the rock and waited for the blood to warm up his hands. Soon he could move his fingers again, and he reached into the leather bag. He pulled out a small bundle, and unwrapped the cloth. In it was some dry dung, some pine resin and flints. Copiously he arranged the dung and resin and lit a small fire by his legs. He reached into the bag again to pull out the pipe. His cold and stiff hand felt something velvety and tender. He pulled out the flower chain and smiled, surprising even himself. Then he pulled out the wooden stem and the red stone pipe. He lifted the stem with his right hand and the bowl with the left, and connected them in reverence just like Guisepe had shown him. The smoking mixture his friend had given him had gotten wet from the rain, but he managed to remember that the original owners of the pipe used tree bark, so he'd scrapped some dry bark off a red birch on his way up. It still seemed dry enough to smoke so he filled the pipe and lit it using a piece of dung from the fire. He was suddenly glad he made it to the peak and felt thankful. It was a strange feeling since he had been so distraught and bitter after her death, their death. If anything he felt betrayed by God, but struggled even with that, acknowledging what he knew to be a man made reaction to that which he could never understand. He knew well that evil happened not because it was the Creator's will, but because He gave us the freedom of our own will and in that space we've managed to kill each other. And yet suddenly he felt thankful for many things, many experiences and opportunities that he encountered in his life, the friendship, the love. He raised the pipe in the air.

'Thank you Great Spirit!' he shouted from his heart. The words and vigour surprised him. He planned to smoke the pipe for his friends, for Guisepe, for Esme, but this was certainly unplanned. 'It has a voice of its own!' he exclaimed, and was suddenly in awe of the sacredness of the object he held in his hands. 'Thaaaank Yoouuu!!!!!!!!' His voice was snatched by the wind instantly but still reverberated in his head. What was happening to him? He felt confused. He thought of Esme and her nonchalant way in dealing with the unexpected. He thought of Guisepe and his deeply grounded faith in all that is good and his clear discernment of what was real. 'I'm dying,' he thought. 'My friends, we'll soon be together again!' he shouted lifting the pipe again. His arms dropped to his legs. His body was going stiff and he couldn't hold them up any longer. His hands were numb now and the cold wind seemed to be blowing now behind his eyes, swirling in the cave of his skull unhindered, a dim light, a lit candle on a piece of wood floating down a dark stream inside the earth.

It was like a dream at first. Through the whispering fog he saw a great brown bear standing on its hind legs – looking at him. In its gaze he felt something of concern and he barely had enough time to decipher his ambivalence when the bear plunged at him. He could see the darkness, feel the water. In it, his skull was tumbling on the pebbles of a shore he couldn't see, kindled by the soft current of a mysterious underground stream. Then nothing. He felt like he was moving in the darkness through the air, moving towards something he couldn't yet see. He saw a soft light in the distance, and heard the sounds of ice melting and water flowing, a springtime warmth chasing away the winter cold. The light was getting brighter. He blinked. He opened his eyes. The morning sun was blazing straight at him and glaring at him from the surface of the rocks around him. The clouds had moved down to the valley. Somewhere in the distance far below he heard a bird sing. He was alive! But . . . how? Why? He took a deep breath and patted his legs with his hands to wake them up. There was something there. He leaned forward. On his legs and the ground all around him were tufts of fur. He picked one and rubbed it with his fingers. Bear! He realised it wasn't a dream . . . the bear had saved him, kept him warm through the blizzard and now was gone. He was alive! Suddenly he felt cheated, deceived. He was meant to die here, he'd seen it in a vision years ago. His love, his friends had gone, he had no reason to exist any longer. He followed his vision and he ends up still alive? Saved by a bear? Why?

The sun was beckoning him to move. He stood up. A few feet ahead of him was the edge, and then a sheer drop through the clouds. Easy. He took a step forward and stopped his foot instinctively losing his balance. 'The pipe! I almost stepped on you my friend. I'll put you away now,' he said as he leaned over to pick it up. He spoke out loud, which surprised him as speaking to himself was not one of his habits. The pipe was still connected. The feeling of Oneness with all life came flooding back through his body, filling him with a nurturing warm feeling as if Mother Earth herself was holding his soul in her bosom.

He found the tattered leather bag on the ground and as he opened it the chain of tiny flowers fell out. He smiled and disconnecting the stem from the bowl he said: 'Ok then. If you won't let me die you'll have to help me live.'

☯

The descent was slow and sweet in the warm sunshine. The steep rock face was home to a few birds, lizards and insects. When he reached the ledge he was in the fog, but it too was thinning out fast from the sun's heat. He thought of the bear cave. In the end he wasn't meant to look for it, he thought, it found him.

Once he came down from the steep rocks he meandered into the woods, looking for a stream or spring. He ended up by the old campfire, which didn't surprise him, so he decided to stay a while, to get some sense of direction for the future. Somehow he felt, it would reveal itself to him, for now he could see his feet moving and he knew he was on the right path.

The next three days he stayed by the old camp. It was late autumn but the weather was good, and there was plenty of wood and water. He discovered many things to eat as well, roots and leaves, bark. He knew how to recognise some mushrooms and ferns, and the use of some bark, but he found that now something had awakened in him a new kind of knowing, a way of asking and listening to what was around him. He spent hours sitting in the clearing just soaking in the sounds and smells, the infinitely varied shades of light that danced through the outstretched passage of time of someone who has died. For that is how he felt, that a part of him had died, and now he was growing another body, out of the mud of the old one. His friends were still there, within his heart, only now there was no pain or fear when he thought of them, only love.

He realised he would never feel alone any more, he had been re-born awake, with the awareness that he was always part of the sacred circle of life. Every moment became something like a prayer, only much deeper, unspoken. The flowers and grasses in the clearings, the ferns, brambles, trees, everything around him became less solid, emitting a colourful light around it, the light blending together like the threads in a carpet, uniting to form a sea of liquid fire. And in this sea his body would melt, losing any sense of boundaries, becoming part of the liquid fire, his mind silently observing, his heart an open white flower on the surface of a still lake without shores, as still as a sheet of ice, as warm as a loved one's embrace.

On the morning of the fourth day, when he went to the spring to drink some water he found his old flask. He'd been to the spring many times in the past days but never noticed it even though it was in plain sight. He filled it up and listened as the spring whispered 'It's time to go!' He walked back to the fire and picked up his leather bag, and wrapped it around itself with some twine to keep it from falling apart. He scattered the leaves erasing any trace of his stay there, thanked the place for its hospitality and headed back south on the trail.

He walked slowly, stopping quite often just to admire a flower, or touch a tree. To watch a bird fly in the sky, or a red squirrel scouring through the fallen leaves for a tasty nut to top off his winter stash.

A few days later the trail had led him close to the hillside farm. He followed his feet on the muddy track leading to the hillside farm's gate. There was a light drizzle in the air, but it was cold and snow not far away. On the western slope by the farmhouse the father and children were all lined up, heads bowed and facing away from him. Next to a heap of soil was a spade stuck in the ground, water dripping off the edge of the wooden handle. Realising they were standing in front of a freshly dug grave he kept silent and approached walking in a circle so that they could see him from a distance. The farmer lifted his arm to acknowledge his presence, and then to signal him to join them. He moved a few steps away from the children to meet him. The children looked at him briefly but stayed in front of the grave.

'My brother, died early this morning,' said the father. John nodded his head but it was devoid of words. 'It was amazing,' he continued, his eyes sparking up as he remembered. 'He'd been so ill for so long, unable even to speak for over a year. After you left, and thank you for the hare by the way, he miraculously recovered. He could sit up even, and talk just fine! We were all amazed, but he told me that he didn't have much time and asked me to get his leather working tools and materials. He stayed up all night working on something, it's for you. Come in the house, I'll get it. Come on children! Time to get out of the rain! Remember what your uncle told you about not crying for him ...' John followed the farmer to the house. He didn't even know their names, but still he couldn't find any words in his head.

The door led straight to the kitchen, and the farmer motioned for him to sit by the large wooden table. John just smiled at him and kept standing whilst he rummaged through the top drawer of a chest. 'Here it is,' he said and handed him a leather bundle. John unfolded it and looked at it stunned. Then he smiled. He put his tattered remains of a leather bag on the table and the new one next to it. They were almost identical! Same size, stitching and design, both with a circle in the middle, with a cross inside it, so similar they could have been made by the same hands. The farmer looked at the two bags and then scratched the chin under his thick beard. Then he turned and offered his hand. 'I'm Pierre, my eldest is Martin, the middle one is Eva, and the boy is François.'

'My friends ... call me John. Call me John,' he uttered uncertain as the words just tumbled out of his mouth. He could hear his voice, but couldn't quite recognise it. Sound had a different quality to his ears, as if it was coming from far away and words seemed almost unnecessary, symbols which attempted to constrain that which is infinite, trying to describe what is beyond comprehension. His feet led him on outside. He stood in front of the grave, holding the bag the brother made. He took the pipe out of its old leather to place it in its new home, but his hands connected it instead. Pierre had joined him and was standing by his side. 'Christian. That's my brothers' name. I know you're not a man of the cloth, but I feel you have truth in your heart, and ...' he pointed to the bag 'I think it would be right if you said a few words.' John nodded. His fingers were already packing the red stone bowl with some bark. He held the pipe by his heart for a while, then kneeling on his left leg he held the pipe so that the bowl touched the ground.

'The Earth takes back your empty shell Christian, and all which is too heavy for you to carry! She's shared her love with you, so many seasons, and her flesh to feed you ...' He stood up and raised the pipe to the sky. Pierre looked on solemnly. The children had crept out of the house and were watching hidden from a safe distance. 'With her love your spirit rises to the heavens, to join the Sun in the true light of the Creator's love ... and with this smoke rise our prayers for a safe journey! We love you! I thank you!' He brought the pipe in front of his heart again and held it there for a while. Then he took it apart and put it in its bag.

'Thank you, that was ... it felt right,' said Pierre. John smiled. He felt he was as much a spectator as Pierre had been during this experience. He looked for his head to try and sort it all out for him, but he couldn't find it. He felt free.

'Christian asked me to thank you for coming this way. He also said something I didn't understand, about taking your place, something about the bag being an offering to the bear. It's made of bear skin by the way, the bag. From the mountains around here.' Pierre looked into John's eyes. They seemed to be looking far away, way beyond where Pierre wanted to go.

'I must leave now,' said John suddenly, looking like a bird on a grassy field that just caught a new smell as the wind shifts and props its wings up slightly ready to fly off. 'Where are you headed?' asked Pierre as he accompanied him to the trail.

'Wherever my feet take me, they seem to know the way,' replied John softly with a smile. Pierre nodded. The children ran up from behind the house and joined their father waving goodbye. John waved back and headed down the hills. He had no idea where he was going, and it didn't bother him.

He just kept walking for weeks, staying close to the southern side of the mountains as he travelled east. He kept away from the towns, and spoke to no one out of the few people he encountered on the way. Most just avoided him, after all he was living like a wild animal and even looked like one by now. He was unarmed but felt no fear, although the threat of violence was sometimes in the air. People looked mostly sad, hard lives and a harsh winter knocking on the door. Yet some were friendly and kind, and they fed him and clothed him even though he did not speak. Ever since he left the hillside farm he couldn't find the words any more. The glowing feeling of stillness he had in his heart was still there, but outside the storm was raging of feelings blowing by, swirling around him, testing his resolve to stay on track. He walked through most of the winter, crossing the one mountain range after the other, until he found a cave where he stayed until the beginning of spring.

'That's when the monks found him and brought him down.' The old monk turned and looked at the monastery. The sun had just set and the big oak gates were groaning from their own weight as they were being closed for the night. He turned and looked at Gregory and smiled. 'Don't worry; we can go to the boathouse to spend the night. There's some food and wood for a fire, and there's even a barrel of wine there.' Gregory looked back at him and nodded, with more questions in his eyes than before. Now, at the end of the narration, he realised that the old monk was speaking the truth to him when he had said that he never told this story before, for he realised that all that he had said would have to be the truth. He was bound by the sacredness he'd touched in his life. Suddenly the gravity of his own role as a witness dawned upon him.

'Why me? Why tell me, a complete stranger, what you've never told anyone ever before?' Gregory was visibly shaken, by the story itself and by the responsibility that he suddenly realised had been placed upon his shoulders. He was scared.

'I knew you were coming Gregory,' replied the old monk placing his arm reassuringly on Gregory's shoulders. 'Just like Guisepe before me I had a bundle to give away, a gift. Only this one isn't wrapped in leather yet, it's a healing story. And I have given it to you because you will write it down for others to benefit from.' The old monk spoke with a calm, knowing voice. He spoke from a place so solid, that the great rocks of this Earth can rest their tired feet on in their seemingly endless journey through life.

'But how do you know I will write it? I mean, I understand why you have kept it under wraps, a lot of it is hard even for me to believe, and I have been searching for the truth with an open mind for years. The monks themselves would certainly be suspicious of your past, they could even turn you over to the Turks, so how do you know I won't tell them?' In his heart, Gregory felt honoured to be trusted, and more than lucky to encounter the healer. His journey had come to fruition, he felt he had arrived, and an important task had been appointed to him. His heart knew, yet his mind had to ask.

'You came here looking for the truth. The truth is like a beach, and I have given you a grain of sand. Every time you let that grain touch your heart it will take you to the beach. You will write the story because this is the task given to you, and your heart won't be able to hold it in for long. Furthermore, you know this to be true. As for the monks, well it doesn't really matter if you do tell them. You see, I'm leaving tonight, there's too much going on here for my liking anyway.' The old monk stood up effortlessly and gazed at the sky as if searching for something.

'Where are you going to go?' asked Gregory, feeling somehow entitled to pry into the old monk's future.

'There are still a few islands further south under the Venetian flag. I'll find some small monastery somewhere out of the way to spend the rest of my days in peace.'

'And the pipe?'

'It goes with me wherever I go. I am the pipe carrier

after all.' The old monk turned and looked at Gregory with a wide smile. He remembered that night in Guisepe's hut when he first lifted the pipe in the air. He knew what the next question would be.

'But as you said, you're retiring, why don't you hand it down? I'm not implying you should give it to me, but someone ... who will use it.' Gregory spoke apprehensively, treading a fine line between his need to know and his fear of appearing greedy. He certainly didn't want the old man to think he didn't appreciate what had been given to him already.

'Oh, I'm not done with it yet – it goes with me all the way. One day it will be needed again, and when the time comes it will be found.'

'Better not hide it too well then. Maybe you should leave a map or some sort of clue, otherwise nobody will know where it is ...' said Gregory.

'I will.' Replied the old monk as he turned his back on him and walked towards the boathouse.

The full moon rose in its glory, taking up most of the sky as it did. A shimmering curtain of silver white light descended from Her and touched the calm waters of the bay giving birth to a narrow ray of bright light that poured through the open boathouse windows. Gregory sat up on his hard bedding and looked outside. A small sailboat carrying a single passenger was making its way out of the monastery's bay and towards the open sea. Inside his heart the story was moving, swirling. He had already decided to stay at the monastery and write the story. There was a library on the top floor, from where you could see nothing but the sea. He would sit there and write, and think of the old monk, Captain Death, or John to his friends. The one who suffered, who was touched by the sacredness of life, who survived, the one who found the healing ways and brought them back down with him.

CHAPTER 12
THE BRIDGE

'Oh please, not more hippy dippy bullshit!' exclaimed Kevin throwing a pamphlet on the table. Andri picked it up and started reading it.

'Hey guys, listen to this, it's quite cool. Written by some old hippy in California. Kevin's a registered cynic, we all know that, but I'll read it for the rest of you ...'

> *"Drugs, from a historical perspective have been used throughout human civilisations, in various ways and forms. Most civilisations have used what nature provides, from stimulants to sedatives, spirits to psychedelics, humanity has learned the uses of plants for medicinal purposes, including spiritual growth. Abuse of any plant can have dire consequences, such as physical death. It is for this reason that their preparation and dispensation was traditionally limited to those who had been called to learn about it all, and undertaken the medicine ways with total dedication. When the medicine person is suddenly substituted by a street vendor looking to make some dough, and anyone can get their hands on anything, then things obviously are quick to decline. Many young ones have lost themselves in that quagmire, many have died.*

I believe that a drug should be judged by its effect, ultimately what does it do to people, and to you specifically. This doesn't mean we should ignore others' experiences, on the contrary. My personal experience led me to quickly realise that people became very weird from the use of the white stuff, and that I didn't like what it did to others. Same with the man made stuff, all speed and generally unbalanced. Are there good and bad drugs? No, but the use of many of these drugs is not good for you, not unless you can overcome them and move on. And psychedelics? One should be ready for them, and guided through their use by one who's been there and seen that movie. So that's the rap from that perspective.

But there is more, like the proverbial onion and its layers. There is a question we could ask and that is why? Why has creation provided us with psychedelics? Why not make it so that we can experience reality like that anyway? Why is there a separation between the world we live in and the spiritual? Why do we need these bridges, like the psychedelics to get there? Well, the answer is that we don't, we don't need the drugs, the rituals, the manifestation. We can still be in oneness with all that is, directly. If you need to have a vision, then you will, and if you are not ready for it, then any amount of drugs won't take you there. It's the truly asking that matters. Yet there is something to be said about manifestation and ritual. Maybe for when we need something, it's there for us anyway. More opportunities, more paths. The variety on this Earth is amazing, and that's how the Great Mystery intended it to be. All these beings, the rocks, the plants, the animals. Of all, we are different, we are the experimentation ground. Something different to sort out for all the beings on this Earth was given to us as humans. Our relations the plants and animals, have changed to adapt to the planet's changes, over long periods of time. And our bodies have also taken similar amounts of time to evolve. But something other than that has led us to experience big rises in consciousness, and catastrophic events to go with that. Yet now, we've come again to cause an imbalance on the Earth, at a much faster pace, as our seeming ability to manipulate the natural environment is ever increasing. Only a miracle can save us now. For whatever happens to us the Earth will go on, and life will grow again. Yet, maybe we are meant to be here. Just maybe, maybe there is a role for us, and that's why all this is happening. Maybe we have a chance, no, more than a chance, a responsibility, to help the Earth heal from all we have made it suffer, all the negative things we've done to all our relations. And if this reasoning is right, and we do have a role to play then to be in tune with the Earth is a prerequisite. If we are not here only for decoration, but to experience the consciousness that being incarnate provides, the meaning of time and cycles, and change, which we uniquely out of our relations have been given, then we must also be uniquely responsible for what happens here.

But to lighten the load, the Great One has given us all the help we could possibly need, in our relations (the rocks, plants and animals), to help and guide each and every one us in the journey on this Earth, and also the protection and guidance of the Ancestors and Guardians.

We can start with the giving of our will to the Great Spirit and opening up, attuning to all that is.

If you are trying you're still in the introduction – don't try, just do it!

Zoroaster Hugging Tree

'First of all how can you take someone with a name like that seriously?' laughed Kevin who had shown great restraint by not interrupting the long banter. 'And secondly . . . well he does have a point about some things, like the sad state of the world, and the responsibility of humans, but that's it. The rest is pure hogwash!' Kevin was never one for mincing his words, direct and in your face was his preferred option.

'To be fair I have to agree with Kevin on this. Zoroaster spells it out nicely but then in two sentences wraps it up with a "give up your will to God" and something about guardians and its all going to be all right. A bit of a leap there . . .' said Thodoras. 'Not that I can see any path from here to utopia myself,' he added as an afterthought.

'Neither can I,' conceded Andri, tossing the pamphlet to the corner of the room. His life had become boring as of late, and he'd lost his will to enthusiastically defend super optimistic outlooks. In the past few years he had changed a lot, he realised that, but now he found himself in a familiar place. It had crept up on him during the summer. A place he knew well, the doldrums of the soul. He had already tuned out of the on going conversation, so he made some excuse about working late and retired in his room. He lay down on the mattress and closed his eyes. Soon he was fast asleep.

The gentle song of a sparrow kissed his ears. He gradually opened his eyes to the soft light of dusk. He looked outside the window. Further up the hillside a group of ravens were perched on the top of the tall pine trees having their usual sunset banter. Groaning he stretched and stood off the hard futon mattress. Slowly, still trying to wake up from dreams he didn't recall, he made his way to the toilet. While he stood there pissing he noticed his watch sitting on top of the short tiled wall that separated the loo from the bath tub. He remembered when he left it here months ago. He'd have a sudden insight, a moment of Satori as he had waited in agony for someone to finish with the loo; after the eventual relief realising that the meaning of time has more to do with how far you are from a toilet when you really need to go, rather than with a couple of metal dials spinning around in a small glass cage. He decided never to wear a watch again.

He went to the kitchen and made a cup of coffee. The house was quiet, nobody about. The birds had finished with their farewell to the sun and the heavy cover of the night's cloak was waving in the sky. Andri lit a cigarette and dragged the smoke deep in his lungs before letting it go. It made him a bit queasy in his stomach. His body didn't want it. He remembered his first serious girlfriend and how she had grabbed his pack of cigarettes one day and thrown them on the street. 'It doesn't suit you, smoking,' she had told him in frustration. She'd told him he was using smoking to hide from his feelings. He knew she was right. 'Tough!' he though out loud. 'It's my life.' Something in his mind pulled out a scene from a film he'd seen, Papillon, the story of a man's thirst for his freedom, which he has been unjustly deprived of by a corrupt legal system, while betrayed by his wife and his lawyer. At some point in the film, the character, played by Steve McQueen and backed by Dustin Hoffman, is delirious, in isolation and has a dream where he walks through a desert and faces the judges who tried him protesting his innocence of the murder he was convicted of. The judges then turn around and tell him that he's not being judged for that, but rather for 'a lifetime wasted' and he leaves saying 'guilty, guilty'.

'Rubbish!' he thought, 'how can I have wasted my life since I don't even know what I'm really here for? I might not be getting any answers, but at least I'm asking the questions.' The walls of the house seemed grey and tall, looming over him like a prison wall. He decided to go out for a walk.

☯

He crossed the avenue and went through the narrow alley between the small factories which led to the railway tracks. The night shift was on and he could see through the dirty glass window panes the workers on the assembly line, neatly packing shirts the one after the other, endlessly. A lone young tree had managed to lift itself beyond the urine stench and the shadows of the factories and had spread its branches over the flat corrugated steel roofs. Andri kicked an empty beer can with his heavy boot and sent it crashing into a pile of litter. The rail tracks were snaking between the back of the factories and the backyards of the houses on the other side. They lay on a muddy strip of land, which became icy and slippery in the winter. The opening in the chain link fence led to the dead end of a side street, and a shortcut down to the river.

It was one of those dark starless nights, and he felt the sadness slowly filling his soul, a stream of water trickling into a pond. This sadness had been in his life as long as he could remember, like the loneliness inherent to every living being. He aimlessly wandered in the empty streets to get deeper into what he felt that had always been there in his life. The air started turning blue around him and he realised he was close to the water. There was thick fog over the river and the running water was playing an entrancing music. He found himself half way across a bridge before he realised he had walked into the fog and was wondering what to do next when he caught a glimpse of something to his left, a distant fire on the shore. He was intrigued so he crossed the bridge and started walking towards the fire. His fears slowly melted away, step by step, as he felt a good feeling growing inside of him, something that was telling him that was where he was intending to go, something deep inside calling him from where he had been to where he was now. The music was faint in the beginning, but then he recognised a guitar, and a violin, and as he got closer he felt the earth move to a rhythmical thumping of a deep drum, a primal beat in oneness with the Earth's heartbeat. There were people around the fire that looked like gypsies with beautiful coloured woven blankets around them, beads and feathers on brightly coloured garments, smiles of wholeness and vibrant eyes. One person came over and greeted him in love, hugged him and welcomed him to the fire. He stood by the fire for a long time dazzled by what he had just experienced. He looked around him. People were playing music, dancing, cooking, tending the fire. The fire was very uplifting, swirling up through the clouds to the heavens. He started meeting people, asking questions. Everybody was from a different place, and nobody knew when the fire began. 'It has always been here, since the beginning,' someone said.

They had all been drawn there by the fire, crossing the bridge. He wandered off. The clouds had parted and the stars' light rushed through the opening like water over a collapsed dam. A memory from a distant past awakened yawning inside of him.

He found himself in the fog again and suddenly it seemed on the other side of the river. He turned around but there was no bridge, and no sign of a fire, only fog. He wondered again aimlessly through the dark streets, but he felt lighter, his sadness pushed aside by a feeling of excitement, of anticipation for the dawn.

When he got back to the house everybody was still asleep or gone. He quietly took his boots off and lay on the bed. His mind was racing, so he picked up his notepad and started writing. He called it a 'mind dump' but sometimes it was the only way to keep his sanity, at least if he wrote things down he had half a chance to keep track of his mental state. A barn owl hooted to announce its arrival at the nest with a fresh killed mouse. He had fallen asleep on his desk. In the middle of the night Thodoras had gently placed a blanket over him. The night slipped away.

In the morning, after a strong cup of coffee and a smoke he went over his notebook. He'd written a few pages in the night, although he couldn't remember what it was all about. He was pretty certain he had gone for a walk down to the river, but the rest, did he dream it? He wasn't sure, but maybe the notes would give him a clue he thought. He turned to the last page he had written and read:

Stream of consciousness
Involuntary convulsions of a new born remembrance of its mother as it runs into the barrier of a dying society accus-

ing its children of no less than more psychological problems of the eternally twisted reality which has not yet been accepted by those who suffered through it yet forgot to remember its unknown murky origins in what created them and what continues to create those forces of excusable social norms from which I cannot derive any substance for nurturing the arid desert in the womb of a rotting jungle of supergrowth contemplating moves of dirty industrial pollutants entering and exiting from the no way out of here rigid petrified process of an organically grown forest of fruitless trees growing leaves underground from ancient times cultivating the wine of deceptive altruism while you sit and stare at what is commonly identified as a self like a naked snail wandering about green rocks formed by the eruptive cavities of expulsive materials coming from the centre of the outside sky inverted into itself forming and simultaneously destroying all that it bears like a seed flying in the air absorbed by a passing cloud and raining into your soul from the trapdoor of no-understanding does it come from the question you answer before I ask where the source is.

Suddenly he felt very alone. His mind was on the edge of a cliff ready for a leap, or was it already too late? The door knocked.

'Hey, Andri, are you still alive?' Thodoras voice came through like a ray of hope on a sinking ship. Andri grabbed the opportunity and opened the door.

'You've just saved me from the quicksand of self pity my friend!' he said jokingly. 'Good' replied Thodoras with a smile. 'Always glad to help a friend in need. Now listen up, I've got good news, no ... great news!' Thodoras was rarely that excited, and by now Nash and

Tom had also come to land in the living room, morning coffee on hand. Thodoras was moving his arms about as if trying to catch some fleeting memory. 'Ah yes …' he started. 'I ran into the old friend of mine down by the square, at the park you know, at the nightime drumming and juggling circle … so anyway he's been travelling around the country, mining crystals and such, and he says there's a big spiritual gathering happening soon in New England! A hippie thing that started in the late sixties in California I think, a real magical place! It's called the Rainbow gathering because it unites people of all colours and religions. And Andri, guess what? You'll love this, it's great!' Thodoras could hardly contain his childlike exuberance and sounded like the guy who opened his back door and discovered a whole new world. 'There's even a Native American prophesy about a last tribe which will emerge towards the end of things, and the name of it is the Rainbow tribe! Now how far out is that?' Thodoras circled the room with his eyes eliciting a response from one of his friends. Nash took another gulp of coffee and put the mug on the wooden power cable spindle which served as a coffee table.

'Sounds great to me. I've heard of these things before, I think, could be something different. Anyway, I say we get organised and go check it out. When is it happening, any idea?'

'Summertime, the main event is on the 4th of July, a prayer circle for world peace. We've got to organise work so we can go for a couple of weeks. I've got to dig out my camping gear …' Thodoras was already packing in his mind.

Andri leaned back on the armchair stretching his back like a cat. 'What do you think about it Tom? You going?' he asked as he slumped back into the green monster – another one of Nash's trash day finds. 'Probably not. Not my kind of thing, a bunch of hippies in the woods. Sounds like a recipe for disaster if you ask me. You go and you can tell me all about it. You can keep your alpha-alpha sprouts and deer ticks, I'll think of you as I'm sipping a nice cold beer and eating a nice succulent steak! Come to think of it I'll be going over to Elsie's café, anyone coming?' Nash nodded, still sipping the endless mug of thick coffee. 'I'll be ready in a minute, or two. Now what was it I needed to do?' He got up and walked towards his room looking intently at the wooden floor, waiting for the answer to his question. Surely enough, a couple of paces later, with a typical 'oh, yes, now I remember' he picked up his normal semi-frantic pace. Andri, like the rest of them, had become so accustomed to their friend's mental habits that he expected it to unfold just like a movie you've seen many times. He shook his head and giggled. Thodoras had completed his mental list by now and had returned to the outside world. 'I expect you are coming to this gathering?' he said looking at Andri, not exactly asking, but more like he was waiting for confirmation. 'You know I will, of course, wouldn't miss it for the world!' he replied patting his friend on the back reassuringly. 'We better get packing then!' he added jokingly.

He hadn't told anyone of his experience the night before, it was all too weird anyway, and he hardly believed it himself. It seemed more of a dream, now that the Sun was out. And yet ... 'Oh no, I mustn't do that!' he murmured to himself covering his eyes with his hand. Thodoras caught the moment. 'What's that?' he asked.

'Oh, just talking to myself ...' Andri was clearly reluctant. He took a deep breath, remembering James's carving of the Sun and Moon. Know yourself! The voice was screaming inside his head.

'Talk to me,' prodded Thodoras. His behaviour was quite unusual as he often spent days in introspection and was very sensitive of other people's space as a consequence. But he was also Andri's good friend, and felt the responsibility to help him develop when it was clear to him that he could. He could feel in this instance that Andri was hiding something from himself, something he had recognised in himself as well – a grey area. Reluctantly Andri came around.

'I mustn't doubt my own experiences. Somewhere inside of me I know my experiences are valid, real, whether I've been taking drugs or not doesn't seem to matter. I know what's real by asking my heart. What the essence of it is. The mind is too limited, emotions too unreliable. But those deeper experiences, they are more real than anything to me. Just sometimes, I kind of wander off to this place where I don't know, I lose faith ... it all seems too much, and too far from what normal society is like. I guess it frightens me a bit. What's normal is far too scary, and what I see as real far too distant.'

'Don't worry man, we're not alone. There's hope in the world, lots of good people out there doing good things

... You'll feel much better about it all when you meet this lot, the rainbows. Really good energy!' Thodoras positive attitude put a smile on Andri's face. 'Well, it certainly seems to have rubbed off on you. Yeah, you're right, we are here to discover, and this does sound like our kind of gig. Should we go meet them at Elsie's, what do you say?'

'Now you're talking! Let's go, I'm starving!' replied Thodoras. Their footsteps echoed through the wooden staircase as they trotted down the steps, down the hill and out onto the main drag.

☯

The early summer days brought much excitement. The anticipation of the trip to the gathering sometimes made the time stretch, especially at work, and other times it would make time shrink, especially the weekends.

The graveyard shifts at the convenience store on Mass Ave were as slow as always. After the onslaught of drinkers grabbing a large sub and assorted junk food after closing time the place would go very quiet for the rest of the night. There was ample time to mop and clear away the deli counter and restock the shelves. Andri liked to sort it all out early and then take it easy, serving the occasional customer, usually a truck driver on the way through town, or some factory worker on the way home.

Chris, who had the next shift, would usually show up half an hour early, to do his 'shopping' as he put it and stash it away in his car before the morning crowd. Andri didn't like it, but couldn't blame him either. The pay was low, and the boss was stingy. He'd never give a discount to the employees, and insisted that the meat for the sandwiches was weighed and was never more than the prescribed amount, which never seemed enough. But the boss only worked days, so Andri would make nice big fat sandwiches, the way he'd make them for himself, that seemed fair enough to him. Needless to say he ended up having some regular customers in the early evening!

The big glass door swung open. A couple walked in, black leathers, gelled spiky hair and metal studs all over. They were both unsteady on their feet, and exuded a feeling like a jagged edge, which made Andri think of crack. He straightened himself up behind the counter. The girl looked really out of it, her dark purple makeup smudged around her eyes, looking like a wet puppy.

'My girlfriend here needs to use the toilet,' said the guy in a slow, low tone. She looked up and pretended to smile.

'Sorry, we don't have a public toilet,' replied Andri. There was a loo of course, but it was stacked up with cartons of cigarettes, as the owner had used up every inch of the store to display things, and cigarettes were always in high demand at night. Andri had a feeling that was the intent of them two anyway. His suspicion was immediately confirmed by the guys reaction.

'I know you've got a toilet, don't fuck with me you asshole!' he screamed in his face. The girl hissed like a vampire that suddenly sees the light and started grabbing at the candy in front of the counter and stuffing it in her pockets. The man, obviously agitated by whatever drugs he was on started shouting even louder and banging on the counter with his fists. 'Give me the fucking money, now!' He wore stubbed leather gloves with rows of steel studs on them and was making quite a mess of the laminated particle board countertop. Andri watched him carefully to see if he was carrying a gun or knife. It didn't seem like he did, and although he was out of it he didn't seem a real threat. 'No, I can't do that, its not mine,' he replied calmly. The man grabbed onto the metal cash register, and amazingly managed to tear it off the counter, leaving four big holes where it had been bolted down. He lifted the heavy thing and with his girl in tow walked out onto the empty avenue, crisscrossing it a few times in his drunken meander. Andri stood there looking at the broken counter. 'I guess I should call the cops soon, and then the boss,' he thought, but before he could lift up the phone a passing patrol car had spotted the couple and had turned the flashing blue lights on. Andri was relieved, not that the perpetrator had been stopped, but that he didn't have to call the cops on him. He called the boss instead, who was soon on the scene in his pyjamas, wide awake in the middle of the night assessing the damage. At the end of his shift, he walked home under the early rising Sun, glad he was but the employee, and didn't have to spend the night stressing out about how to replace the register and get some wood for the countertop, fill the insurance forms in and all that crap. Not his responsibility.

A few yards along a side street off the avenue inside a small front yard of a white colonial house a ray of morning light caressed the sleeping blossom on a young apple tree. What was his responsibility in life, why was he really there? He asked himself that question for as long as he could remember, but recently things had changed. Now he was praying for an answer. Now he was ready to know.

CHAPTER 13
RAINBOW TIME!

'Let's see, tent, sleeping bag, clothes, pipe, smoke, money. Flashlight. Ok.' Nash zipped his rucksack up again and threw it unceremoniously in the trunk. 'We're ready to rock and roll!' he declared. Thodoras and Andri had already climbed in and waving goodbye to the small group of friends who were staying at the house as they made their way onto the main drag and towards the Turnpike. 'West all the way and then we dip into Pennsylvania,' said Thodoras, holding up the map. 'Looks like a good six hours drive if we don't stop too often, its all the way into the mountains. Can't wait!' The Talking Heads were blaring through the speakers filling the small car with sound, mixing with the smoke from the pipe that Andri had lit in the back as he declared his feelings with a long eeehhaa! Like some urban cowboy on the highway.

The hours passed, the drivers switched around, large coffees to go and many miles later they were driving around the Alleghany mountains. It was mid day and they were concerned about finding the site in the dark.

‘Where is it exactly?’ asked Nash who was on the steering wheel.

‘Well, on this hand drawn map here it’s between route six, route sixty six, and 666. How weird is that?’ commented Thodoras.

‘Yeah, spooky. But how do we find this place?’ insisted Nash.

‘There’s a little heart here close to this corner. We should be looking for a “welcome home” sign.’

Nash breathed out in frustration. Then he suddenly perked his eyes and slammed onto the brakes. The car slid for a few yards on the dirt road. ‘There!’ he said. ‘We just passed it.’

‘Good eyes man,’ commented Andri from the back. As the car reversed they saw a bunch of stones piled up under a small wooden sign painted with a rainbow and pointing up the small forest track. A few coloured ribbons were tangled up in the branches of the tall pine tree. They followed the track to another sign, another turn and then a long wide logging road full of neatly parked cars. They found a space and parked, and poured themselves out of the car in relief after the long journey. They had barely stretched and looked around when an old hippy jumped out of the brush. He had long white hair and beard, and he stood naked in front of them holding a tray of fruit in his hands.

‘Welcome home brothers! Have some lovely melon! I’m Om, and here’s the rap!’

Rap 107

The three friends looked at each other with smiling eyes, and they dug into the juicy melon whilst Om, who had apparently spotted some old friends, meandered off between the cars. The trail was obvious but also marked by a small rainbow sign and coloured streamers. Soon they were trekking up the hill, surrounded by a beautiful hardwood forest mixed with great stands of tall pine trees. The growth on the ground was clear evidence in support of its naming – a deciduous rain forest. The parked cars were quickly swallowed up by the rampant green growth. The trail was well walked on, and parts of it that were naturally muddy had already been layered with thick branches to prevent erosion. On the steepest part of it a thick rope had been tied to a big pine tree and laid on the side of the trail, to help people with heavy loads. For a while they walked in silence, absorbing the sounds of the forest, decompressing from the long journey, the city. The trail dipped along the side of a steep valley, unwinding along the naked skin of the Earth. About 100 yards away was a group of people headed towards them, dancing and giggling. As they came close, they shouted out 'Hug patrol!' and proceeded hugging the three friends in a big group hug. 'Welcome home!' they declared and danced away singing, 'We love you!'

'Wow, feel that energy, this is great!' declared Nash with the enthusiasm of a child just past the gates of the amusement park.

'Yeah man, and we haven't even got there yet! Let's move on!' replied Thodoras, anxious to get closer to the action. They followed the trail through the woods, and started to encounter various camps along the way. These usually consisted of groups of tents and tarps set up in the vicinity of a central tarped area, with a kitchen. Some of these were elaborate structures, using the surrounding trees and some wooden structure made of long branches and tree trunks. Large pots and five gallon plastic buckets, sacks of potatoes, beans and rice, bags of fresh vegetables all neatly stacked. It all pointed to the communal living, like the villages of old, or even more like a bunch of tribes.

They found an area they liked, next to the butterfly camp, and they pitched their tents. Thodoras was soon off down the trail, looking for some camp or other where he knew somebody. Nash was next to plunge into the gathering, so he wandered off, came back, rummaged around his tent and was off again mumbling about something he mustn't forget. Andri lay in his tent for a while, soaking in the sounds of the forest mixed in with voices of happy people. It all started to sound like a song, like the melodic babble of a slow running stream over smooth round rocks. As he came back to himself he felt his heavy heart. There was a longing in him for companionship, it had been over a year now since his last serious relationship. But he also recognised a deeper need, a more essential longing, that of his spirit. It so wanted to fly, to be close to the Great Spirit, but it was held back. A web of feelings kept it pinned down, a lethal mix of sorrow, fear, pain, anger, self doubt and self pity. It was all tangled up inside his soul, and he prayed for one day to be able to slash the knot like Alexander of Macedonia. In the meantime he had to accept it and find the inner strength to keep going. Where his life was leading to he wasn't sure, but now he was here, a good place for healing, a place that felt like home.

He picked himself up and wandered around, silently

observing the people meandering about between the various camps and the main fire. There were hugs and happy encounters all over. A beehive of activity as well. People were carrying supplies, cooking, digging, setting up camps, improving trails, helping each other. For a bunch of hippies there was a lot of work going on. He passed a figure sitting on the roots of a big tree. He held a piece of wire in front of him and was showing a long braided girl as he twisted and turned it. In one smooth continuous motion he moved his hands and produced a lovely butterfly, with swirls on the edges of its wings.

'Here you go sister,' said the man.

'Thank you brother, its lovely!' she replied and gave him a warm hug. 'What's your name?' she asked as she was leaving.

'Butterfly Jack!' he smiled.

Andri walked along. He was impressed by the butterfly, but somehow the whole scene made him feel more alone. He recalled a spring he passed earlier on and decided to go and fill his water bottle. As he got there, he encountered a tall man leaving the spring. He was wearing some kind of animal skin vest and jeans. A bunch of necklaces were dangling on his chest, and feathers hanging from his long hair. They smiled at each other. Andri crouched over to fill his bottle and found a necklace on the wet stones. He turned around quickly and called at the man.

'Excuse me ... I think this belongs to you,' he said holding it up. It was a butterfly, a butterfly Jack job.

'Well, it's yours now. It obviously wanted to be found ...'

'Why ... thank you brother,' said Andri, 'I'm Andri ...'

'I'm Sun Bear,' replied the man, and gave him a big bear hug.

The main trail widened under the tall branches of the maple trees. Like a river it opened up just at the edge of the grassy field leading to the main circle. Food circle had already finished, he'd heard the massive AUM as he was coming down from the spring. The many tribal kitchens, at least 50 and maybe up to 70 was his best estimate so far, had synchronised their activities – in hippie time of course- and amazingly managed to serve out enough food to feed the at least ten thousand gatherers. All ages were there, from newborn babies to white haired granddads and grandmothers. All colours, shapes and sizes of people had gathered, a real tribal thing, alternative and colourful, positive and loving. The energy that went into the place had already impressed Andri, and soon enough he discovered the urge to get involved and do things for others, for all. These people were his brothers and sisters, searching spirits conscious of the 'we're all on the same boat' reality of things. Artwork had sprung up everywhere around the forest it seemed, from stone sculptures along the creeks, to huge spider webs in the middle of the woods, colourful banners and big painted wooden signs.

Now, around the main circle fire, a small circle of people were having some kind of debate, although they took turns in talking by passing around a talking feather. Someone was announcing some sort of plant walk through the woods, for anyone interested in learning about the edible plants in the rainforest. Meditation and chanting at the crystal tepee by fairy meadow at sundown was another thing going on. Like a big beehive, the whole area was buzzing with seemingly coordinated activity. Some unseen force had created close to perfect harmony out of what should have been total chaos.

By the time he got in his sleeping bag, Andri was exhausted from the many experiences and the hours in the car, trekking up and down the hills, and helping with the supply chain to the kitchens. The drumming from the main circle was humming through the trees, a tribal beat of over 100 drums and all sorts of percussion instruments – many handmade – accompanied by wind instruments, he could make out a clarinet and a saxophone. Close to the circle you could feel the earth vibrate, but in the woods the music tumbled through, dancing its way through the trees, carrying the pounding of the dancers' feet on the clay soil. Although it was July already the forest was damp and the water in the night air found its bed in the leaves of the trees and the grasses, even the tarps and tents. He felt warm in his sleeping bag, and the feeling of the Earth on his back beckoned him to the arms of Morpheas. The warm sensation in his chest lapped like an ocean wave onto the floating icebergs hidden in the shadows. He hoped he would dream of the Earth, as he floated off to the stars.

The next morning he woke up to the sounds of someone clattering some pots and pans, in the effort of making coffee. The bright sun pierced through the dense trees from high above. The dawn had long gone, and the protecting cover of dense growth had yielded the sleeping moisture to the strong heat of the Sun. Andri rolled a cigarette, and making sure he had his cup with him this time, he walked down the trail in search of some breakfast.

Before he got to the next kitchen he was beckoned over by a couple of guys cooking eggs on a small fire nestled between their two tents. Soon he was sipping some nice coffee, and slowly waking up. In front of him was a man in his forties, slim and pale, wearing a cowboy hat with the southern star on it.

'How do you want your eggs bro?' he asked in a quiet voice. Andri had the impression that it was more of a sore throat from too much hollering rather than his quiet disposition that gave him that mellowness.

'Whatever's easy. Medium I guess is great,' replied Andri sipping on his coffee. He had his back turned to the trail so he didn't see them coming 'till they were there right next to him. Two men in their thirties, wearing suit trousers and waistcoat, white shirts buttoned up all the way. The one who looked older was short, dark short haired, and was already speaking. The other one was slim and tall, and stood a couple of paces behind and to the right of the speaker. He was holding out a big bible, and was reading it out in a slight whisper, like a subliminal prayer.

'We've come to bring the good news! About our Lord Jesus Christ, our saviour! In Him we are reborn, and we are saved from our sins!' Andri thought that the man had obviously done this before, although probably not in these kind of surroundings. These two stuck out and looked so much out of place that he was about to laugh, when the southern man stood up, frying pan with eggs in hand, and burst out at them.

'Good news? My wife joined you born again lot and walked off, brainwashed like a zombie! You save yourselves but do it away from here or you'll have this pan on your head! Piss off!' He sat down as the two 'Christians' made a hasty retreat down the main trail. The cook burst out in laughter, and his friend and Andri joined in.

'Sorry about that bro, I think these eggs are more on the well done side, but here you go anyway . . .' he said and sat down on the log. 'She did just take off, they find unhappy and unbalanced people like her and promise them heaven, then they just suck them in. One day they'll spit her out, and I'll have to pick up the pieces. That's why I get so pissed off, even here they won't leave us alone.'

A couple of days later as Andri was coming back from the sweat lodge, he ran into the tall guy again. They met as they were crossing over a creek, on a bridge made out of a large fallen tree and some rope and branches. He wasn't holding the bible anymore, no waistcoat, and his white shirt was muddy, half hanging out of his trousers.

'How's it going man, managed to save anyone yet?' asked Andri with a smile.

'No, no one seems to want to be saved around here,' he replied sheepishly.

'How about your friend?'

'Oh. He couldn't take it he said, hopeless hedons he said. He left yesterday. I kind of like it here though anyway, so I think I'll stay a bit longer!' said the man. He looked more like little boy now and was smiling.

'Well good luck then. Have fun!' replied Andri. 'There's still hope for you,' he thought, and it made him smile again.

The sky darkened and it started to rain, softly at first, then hard of for a while. Andri found some space under a big blue tarp.

‘It’s going to rain for a while, we might as well have some fun.’ The voice came from a southern looking bloke, wearing a red baseball cap with Texas written on the brow. Three others were huddled around him as they shared a pipe. The man with the hat passed the pipe to Andri. He nodded and took a puff.

‘The wizard is around tonight, I’ve seen him earlier,’ said the man as he took back the bowl. ‘Some great stuff, really clean,’ he added. A couple of hippie girls joined the group. It was still coming down hard, and they looked thoroughly soaked. They both wore jeans and were wrapped in pretty Indian shawls. They sat around and livened up the party instantly. One of them approached Andri and asked him for a cigarette. He offered her one and she sat next to him and smoked. She said her name was Sparrow. Andri felt slightly edgy. Beautiful women often made him feel uncomfortable, and it had been a long time since the last time. Her energy was warm, and soon he felt closer and started interacting a bit more. Another figure popped out of the rain. He was tall, with a long white beard, wearing a rain poncho and a tall pointed white hat. He held a honey coloured staff, tall with a quartz crystal on the top.

‘Open your mouths if you want a dose,’ he said in a husky voice. He sounded like a man on the go with little time to spare. Andri made a quick decision and opened his mouth wide. The white wizard pulled out a eye drop bottle and dropped a few drops of liquid acid on his tongue. The effect was almost instant. Andri felt the heat, and noticed the sudden glow of sparkling surfaces, the dance of light unfolding around him.

The rain had stopped and the sound of water was now a soft dripping from the wet leaves onto the ground. She asked him if he had a flashlight. He did. She asked him if he could help her get to her tent to get some dry clothes. They wandered off into the trees. The tent was not far. It was a good size dome tent, big enough to sleep three or four. A colourful blanket was laid on the floor, and fine silk and cotton materials in red shades draped the sides of it. She took her clothes off and slid under a blanket. They lay there for a while, kissing and fondling each other, and then as if a line had been reached she pulled away and got dressed.

'Things to do, see you later!' she said and she was off into the forest. Andri felt a pang inside. He'd been there before, and it made him reflect about his weird karma with women. 'I better not get into this mind space,' he told himself, well aware of the pitfalls of the mind when tripping. He wandered off towards the main circle, the big fire. The waves from the acid were getting stronger and closer together. He stumbled out of the woods onto an open field on the edge of the main gathering site. Trampling along the mud in the dark, his knees gave in and he fell. Kneeling on the ground he felt the darkness around him change. A purple fire was crackling through the air, like a lightning bolt, giving off white sparks. The air smelt burnt. He changed. He was a black man now, wearing something like a straw dress. The ground around him was parched, the grass burnt out yellow, crumbling into dust to be carried off by the wind. A large horned animal skull lay half buried in the red sandy soil. The land was barren, unyielding. On his erect manhood was a conical shape made of strips of wood, like a hat. He stuck it in the ground making a hole, and stuck his penis in, making love to the earth. Then there was darkness. He could hear the faint sound of voices from far away. The words swam into his ears.

'Too many drugs, not enough sex. That's what I say.'

'Yeah, kids nowadays, there so deprived compared to how we were. It's all so complicated now, AIDS and all the social alienation ...'

A bright light appeared as the sky opened up at the top of his head. He felt elated.

'Look, he's shaking ... wow! ... can you see that?'

'Yeah ... he's bathed in a blue light..'

'He's still shaking a lot, here pass me that blanket, I'll wrap it around him ...'

'Let's bring him by the fire ... careful, his eyes have turned in ...'

'The Angels are coming! The Angels are coming ...' Andri opened his eyes. He was sitting on a log by the main fire, wearing a blanket. A couple of people were snuggled up to him. One of them, a middle aged woman, raised her head and looked at him. Her eyes were warm and reassuring, her smile serene.

'Did I say that?' asked Andri blinking his eyelids trying to focus.

'You have been, for a few minutes now. I hope you don't mind us sitting here, you've got this beautiful energy glowing from inside.' The darkness of the night had just departed, giving way to a soft, soul warming dawn. Some early rising pagans were out already welcoming the rising Sun, in prayer, chant, movement. Someone was swinging a spiral plastic tube creating an eerie cosmic sound. The sky was starting to become ablaze with streaks of colours, yellow, and red, purple, blue climbing on the thin high clouds. The chorus of birdsongs filled the expectant air with a good dose of packed beauty creating another dimension to the intricate tapestry of creation.

Later that day, Andri sat with Nash and Thodoras around a small kitchen fire close to their tents.

'So what happened with you last night? Thodoras mentioned something about a vision.' Nash filled his mug with coffee. 'Where's the milk, do you know?'

'Here, its in this cooler.' Thodoras passed the milk to Nash.

'All I can tell you is that I was taken up, and'

'Taken where?' asked Nash.

'The Sky. And I met a ... very old white haired holy man, and he told me that I was brought up there so I can come back and tell the people that the Angels are coming.' Andri spoke the words almost trembling from the memory of the experience. It was in a strange way similar to when he'd accidentally electrocuted himself fiddling with a table lamp. It was back when the fuses were simple wires, and it took a while to break the current by which time there was smoke coming from the top of his head. Only this time the current was both more gentle and immensely more powerful at the same time.

'The Angels? And when is that going to happen then?' Nash had bad eyesight when tripping, so any picture painting was fruitless. Andri remembered.

'When the stars in the sky change, that's the sign, that's when the Angels will come.'

'Hmm. Yeah, that's cool. I wonder what it all means? Good acid then?'

'Acid? Oh that. No, this wasn't a hallucination, it was more than real ... sacred.' Andri lowered his face into his mug. He rolled a cigarette and blew the smoke around. Who would believe him? If he had heard someone else talk like that a few years ago he'd laugh and blame the drugs. But now, this was different, like the visions of his childhood. He recalled the blue white light that poured in from the top of his head. There was something very familiar about the quality of that light, something deep inside his childhood that resonated with it, that had felt it and knew it well. He couldn't quite place its origin. 'Oh well,' he thought, 'when the time is right I'll know. When the stars change ...'

☯

The next few days flowed by in relative calm. Apart from the 'Christians' he'd met at the start of the gathering, there were few who stuck out. One group was the Krishna's, who paraded around the fields dressed in their orange robes, drumming and chanting. Strangely, they seemed very much at home with the forested terrain and the thousands of colourful hippies. Unlike the 'Christians' they weren't trying to save anyone, but rather enjoyed advertising their belief. They were talking about bringing a small elephant from one of their farms, for the kids.

The other, thankfully small group, was the white robed, imitation leather sandaled holier than thou purists, who pranced about the place in small groups typically criticising the baseness of the situation whilst planning the next 'amazing' purification ritual that would top all other spiritual activity in the gathering. Amazing was more the fact that they kept an incredible large supply of clean white robes in their camps, and that they never seemed to do any physical work. This intellectual elitist attitude disgusted Andri, who thought the least of them. At least the rainbozos, first comers and inexperienced and typically with the mistaken idea that there is a festival type of central organisation that will provide, so they come ill prepared, without even tents or blankets, they often quickly catch up and do some work. As for the white robed rituals, they'd be just words, without any power. In the monasteries in Greece, the monk who does the midnight mass, the most esoteric and powerful, is the one who cleans out the latrines the day before, to ensure humility. Humility was certainly lacking here!

At the end Andri gravitated towards where he felt most comfortable, the teamwork experience of a rainbow gathering kitchen. His experience of the vegan white robes spurred him to join the only meat kitchen in the gathering, Taco Mike's.

"*Taco Tavern. The only second class joint in town*". The sign had been written in neat calligraphic letters above a red painted rose. It was nailed on a wooden post, part of the solid structure that held up the large blue and green kitchen tarps. An assortment of herbs was hanging from the rafters, including a bunch of red hot chillies. Behind them, was a man wearing a leather broad rimmed hat, with feathers and coloured threads. Its occupant was a thin and scraggly man in his thirties, bit shorter than average, wearing a cotton shirt, light blue, jeans and heavy boots. His dark beard had a few grey hairs, but did little to hide his sullen cheeks. He had a roll up in his mouth, hanging from the one corner. He stood by a metal coffee pot helping the coal centre under it with his boots. He looked at Andri through the drying herbs and took the cigarette from his lips, pulled some of the wet tobacco off the end and threw it on the small fire.

'We're not open for breakfast yet amigo, and no you can't help yourself to cooking unless I know you and you're a part of my crew., and I've never seen you before so good day!' he said. His voice sounded like he'd been singing all night, very loudly, and his stance spoke volumes of how he didn't like being bothered in the morning, and didn't want strangers messing about in his kitchen. Andri kept himself from laughing and ended up in a wide smile.

'Did I say something funny?' asked the man sharply.

'No, not at all. Just that I recognised a kindred spirit there. I don't like dealing with people in the mornings either,' replied Andri. 'Anyway, I'll leave you in peace, I'll come back later,' he added and turned to go.

'Well, I'll be making some porridge soon, so . . .'

'Oh, I'm not hungry really, never eat in the mornings usually anyway. I was looking to help out in the kitchen, that's all.'

'Well, why didn't you say so in the first place? I'm Taco Mike, and this is Taco Tavern, the only meat kitchen in the gathering, so as long as you don't have a problem with that you're welcome to help,' he said in a softer tone.

'No problem, I love meat,' replied Andri. 'I'm not

hungry, but if you're making coffee I'd love some,' he added.

'Sure, grab a log for the fire and come sit down. I'll show you what the set up is later ...' they both turned to the sound of a someone scrambling out of a tent close to the kitchen area. A woman emerged and slowly made her way towards Taco Mike. She snuggled next to him and gave him a big kiss.

'Good morning,' she said. 'I hope Taco hasn't been growling too much, he hasn't had his breakfast yet ...'

'This is Rose,' interrupted Taco. 'And, no, I've been very polite ... so far! This unsuspecting victim here wants to join our kitchen ...'

'I wouldn't recommend it!' she interjected. 'The cook has a bad temper, even worse habits, not to mention his bedside manners ...' she laughed as he coughed and grunted loudly straightening his back as if in protest.

'Sounds like the food will be good then ...' replied Andri and got his tobacco out to roll a cigarette. 'And I heard rumours of meat, so the holier than thou white robes won't be hanging around here, which is always good ... want a smoke?' Andri offered the pouch over.

'Hey, I like this guy already; here have some coffee.' Taco poured the thick dark liquid into the black metal cup. He had a wide grin on his face like a naughty child ready to let his mates in on a secret. 'And if you keep it low profile, I've got some bacon here I'm going to fry, enough for the three of us ... real food!'

'Mmmm, bacon! Now you're talking!' replied Andri smacking his lips purposefully. 'And while you do that I'll get some water on the go for the porridge, I can hear people waking up ...' he added as he looked around for a big pot. The kitchen was well organised and already mostly built, apart from what looked like the foundation for a stone and clay oven on the one side of a second cooking fire pit. The pits were well built with stone, covered by large steel grids. There were a few grids on two main fire pits, and not two were remotely similar, salvaged as they were from some industrial machinery or put together by someone with a welding torch using construction rods. There were various wooden racks and shelves for the pots and pans, the washing stations and food storage. A wooden table made of plywood on a stone and wood base served as the main prep area for cutting and mixing. A blue hose stuck through the frame around the back.

'Water's over there.' Taco pointed to the blue hose in the distance. Andri was by the pots trying to decide which one to use. 'Yep, seen it, thanks ...' he replied and picked up a pot big enough to make porridge for 50. He squatted on the ground by the hose waiting for the spring water to fill the pot and looked around. The morning sun was gently finding its way around the meadows and through the trees on the woods. A warm summer day was beginning and thousands of people would soon be moving about, collecting the nectar of good feelings and altruistic actions, for the feast of the spirit and the dance of the night. Andri felt he landed, and there was nowhere he'd rather be more than where he was.

The porridge – fortified with honey and raisins and spiced with cinnamon was a success, especially with the kids. Although he hadn't interfered with Andri's concoction, he was aware that Taco was observing him quietly. In the early afternoon he asked Andri to join in with the building of the oven, and they worked hard all day to get it finished. Andri helped as the kitchen crew continued the work they had began a few days earlier. The oven was made of stone and clay and was shaped like a dragon. The body of the beast was the oven itself, and the neck and head the chimney. It had the traditional triangular mane, and when it was lit smoke and flames poured out of its mouth; a piece of art under a blue plastic tarp. The oven came to its own, when in an amazing display of planning, group effort, co-ordination and sheer arrogance the Taco kitchen produced real tacos for the gathering. The dragon was working overtime, huffing and puffing nicely as a group of a dozen or so volunteers danced around baking, filling, chopping and serving. The wonder of it all was that this kept going for most of the day, feeding what looked at some point to be an endless queue of people.

Taco taught Andri all about rainbow kitchens and they ended up working together at a few gatherings. For Andri he was the 'captain' in the woods, the self sacrificial true human. His medicine came in the form of massive feedings and worked its own magic in the gatherings. Most of the 'older hippies' would find Taco's kitchen first and then decide where to set up. Knowing the man they would often bring some meat, spices and various delicacies. Taco's was the heart kitchen for the down to earth high spirits – the real folk. Being the only meat kitchen in the gathering it also attracted a fair amount of criticism, and the 'wars' with the vegan only kitchens added spice and many funny moments to the whole experience.

There was the incident with the dead chicken for instance. It was at a gathering in Vermont, and the Taco kitchen was high up close to the springs and away from the beaten path. Supplies were more of an issue because they had to be hauled uphill for a mile from main supply. The vegan kitchen was close to main supply and they tended to build a good stock, helping themselves first to the daily supply runs. By the time the Taco crew got down there was often little left. Taco went down himself and complained to the vegan kitchen cook Freddie about the situation, and they begrudgingly conceded some of their supplies, complaining how the gathering was meant to be vegetarian only, and that this 'pirate' kitchen should not even be. A few nice words were exchanged between the two men and the war was on!

The next morning when the Taco crew got to main supply most everything was gone. The vegans claimed innocence, and they were low on rice and beans, and potatoes as well. At night, a special mission from Taco's discovered sacks full of food hidden under tarps behind the vegan kitchen and 'liberated' some of it. A day went by and in the night the vegans nailed a dead chicken on the main post of Taco's kitchen. The crew got together and devised a plan. Late at night they stole into the vegan kitchen and buried the chicken corpse, which by now was smelling very ripe, a few inches deep, on a spot where it wouldn't be stepped on. The heat of the day brought an awful stench, which just kept getting worse. It took them days to find the source of it, and Taco and the crew couldn't stop laughing throughout! The kids were playing and having good fun.

But even in temporary utopia all wasn't rosy. Society's ills didn't just disappear, and not everybody there was searching for enlightenment. From complex 'mental' illnesses to basic medical needs, it was all there to be dealt with. For some illnesses there was alternative medicine, with many practitioners at hand at the MASH medical centre. Without a doubt, the healing energy of the gathering did a lot for the ailing spirits of the gatherers. And that was the important bit. But some of the gaping holes that the 'national healthcare system' presented were more difficult to negotiate.

Case in point was the issue of teeth. Taco Mike spent a big part of one of the gatherings in his tent, suffering from an abscessed tooth, refusing to leave the kitchen and the gathering to go to town to the dentist. It turned out that firstly he didn't have the money for a dentist's visit, and as it wasn't in his nature to ask for help from his friends it took a while until those around him realised what was going on. Essentially however he valued the gathering so much above himself that even when the money was available to him he waited until the days of clean up, at the end of the gathering, to leave the kitchen for a couple of days and have his tooth extracted.

The issue of teeth kept coming up. It was the middle of the night, back at the Pennsylvania gathering, and Andri was hanging out by a fire in front of the big MASH tent. Both mainstream and alternative practitioners used MASH as their centre, and there was always someone available to help. Andri had wandered in, and tended the fire. It was early days and the drumming and dancing around the main fire had ended early on, most of the gatherers resting from all the activities of the day. The clouds had thinned out, and the clear starry night quickly soaked up the heat of the day. Andri threw another log on the fire and stoked it up. A woman appeared from under a blanket and asked him if he needed anything. Her name was Sara, and she was a medical doctor who also practiced alternative healing methods. The rest of the night crew were snug in their sleeping bags and stirred in the one corner of the big white canopy tent. Andri whispered back that he was fine, and asked if he could make some coffee.

'Sure, the kettle's down there ...' she replied in a yawn, 'I'll join you for a cup, the milk is in that cooler by the side there ...'

Andri stepped outside and placed the kettle on the fire grate. MASH was well placed, off the main circle but central to most camps. It was on what seemed as an island, with a couple of deep creeks running around it. Behind it was the path leading to the sweat lodge, on the edge of the dense woods. In front of it, beyond the creek, lay a big open meadow leading to the main circle. The melody of laughter vibrated through the moisture laden air from the edge of the meadow, overriding the gargling water.

'These bloody hippies, always having fun! What's wrong with these people?!' commented Andri raising his hands. Sara giggled. The sound of laughter was coming closer, and soon they could discern two figures coming down the path, waving a flashlight around – mostly missing the ground as if they were trying to illuminate the night sky. At first they seemed like two happy drunks holding on to each other as they wobbled along, but when they came closer they looked much more bizarre than that. Two large framed, middle aged bearded hippies, one with his hand inside the other's mouth, stood on the other bank in front of the big log bridge. They were laughing so hard there were tears in their eyes.

'Ummff, wash it, don't thlip!' said the one with the hand in his mouth.

'This is a good one! Slippery log, here we come! Hold on tight, don't worry, I've got you . . .' replied the other. Sara and Andri helped them across and sat them by the fire. It took a while to get the story, they were still laughing so hard, but as it turned out one of them, Ben, had a loose filling and in a moment of madness conceded to let his friend Howdy glue it back with super glue. The result was that Howdy got his finger glued to Ben's tooth, and they had to make their way down the trail in that state to get help. Only they couldn't stop laughing, which made it even more of a trip! Eventually Sara came up with the solution, and using some dental floss managed to disconnect the two friends. Ben, released from the constraining hand, hollered and rolled on the ground laughing for a few minutes and joined by some of the crew who had gotten out of their sleeping bags to see what all the commotion was about. The jovial atmosphere lasted – with the help of some coffee – all through the dark night.

Inevitably, the gathering came to a close, and people started drifting away. For many it was the trip back to Babylon, back to work and mainstream society, carrying the light of the experience back with them, to nurture and heal until the next time. For some the road led to another gathering, a regional on turtle island, or some rainbow in some other part of the world. For others it was the empty streets and the backpack they always carried.

The clean up had started and as the camps started disappearing one by one; those staying started co-ordinating the recycling, the filling up of the latrines, the seeding of the paths. Like in the beginning there were hundreds, not thousands, but by now the land had taken its toll, and it was time for restoration and preparing the forest to resume its pre-gathering rhythm. Anticipation and excitement had given way to thanks giving and reflection.

Home. The strong feeling was still harboured in Andri's heart. He'd never felt so much at home anywhere else. The prospect of returning to the city almost frightened him, and yet as the forest took over once again it felt inevitable. He tried to find what it was that made him feel that way. It was welling from deep inside, and extended way beyond the temporal limits of the rainbow gathering, a feeling of a timeless experience, a sacred space. Although there was always going to be someone who stumbled through in the darkness and saw the whole thing as a weird camping experience, for the vast majority the gathering was a place to be in balance with nature, focused on the higher energy of universal love. This stretching peace gave such amazing freedom! Freedom from the eons of barriers the established religions had raised, from the twisted minds and plotting gangsters, the lies and bigotry of the mainstream. Deep inside his heart he had felt a joy he couldn't yet identify or even start to describe. It had to do – he felt – with living the real life, walking as spirits on the Earth focused on what is of essence, the way life should be. And close to that was another strong feeling, intense anger, for being deprived the real life for so long. And for how much longer? The thought made him shiver in rage at the edge of desperation, and like a fish out of water he struggled to breathe. He managed to centre himself somewhere in between the warmth of joy and the heat of anger, reciting in his mind the mantra of faith, that all will be well in the end, even if he can't see the path at present. He'd realised the short term nature of utopia. Sure, there were nomads amongst the rainbow, who went from gathering to gathering, and all sort of havens of good people in between, so the energy kept flowing, as it has through the ages in many forms. But it was a temporary space, not a permanent solution, and always at odds with the society around it in one fundamental way or another. The people had been cut off from the land for hundreds of years now, and it was a long and hard way back. In the meantime there was Babylon to contend with.

A few days earlier, whilst on his way down the main trail he had heard someone crying. The sound came from around the bend, so he had approached quietly and stopped just behind a large tree on the side of the trail. From the edge of the large dark brown tree trunk he recognised a couple of people he'd met dancing around the main fire at the peak of the gathering. A teenage girl named Hope, full of life and a great smile, and her mother Karen. Disturbingly, Hope was crying on her mother's shoulder as she was trying to console her gently stroking her hair.

'What about us now?' she said, tears streaming on her tender face. 'Where are we going to go now?'

‘Hush now, it will be all right,’ replied her mother, ‘we’ve survived the streets before, we will again. Until the next time. Don’t cry baby, please . . .’

For the duration of the gathering the woods was everyone’s home. Everything before and after was almost irrelevant, as the energy manifested brought a glimpse of a higher reality. The communal and sharing nature made it so, and people leapt into the love bath and recharged their batteries. And many good friendships were started and people did network and helped each other beyond the gathering time. But the problems are huge in society, and central to the existing way of living. The rainbow was not the solution, he realised that; but it was a space to try to make the dream come true, even in a small way, even the one seed.

CHAPTER 14

GUARDIANS

'I get a feeling, a feeling deep inside, oh yeah!' (Andri to the tune of James Brown). 'You know, I do get a feeling about this, after all the evidence is everywhere, this isn't the first time.'

'Mmm hhh,' Thodoras was struggling with a bunch of rope, trying to unravel it in preparation for the next climb. 'Whoever threw this rope in the corner under the stairs there sure did a good job! This monster has taken a life of its own, aargghh!' Nash was making notes of something, probably something to do with his epic poem he was working on. It was one of those projects that start out of seeming nowhere, and last a lifetime. He slowly lifted his head, as if to make sure he was still writing what he had glimpsed earlier, whilst his mind had obviously jumped to the next concept. 'Do tell us then, what are you mumbling about?'

'Well, on the one hand we have all this archaeological evidence of ancient civilisations, more cropping up all the time, big settlements with big structures, most involving some type of pyramid or other temple at the centre, inhabited for a good number of years, and then gone, abruptly, which kind of points to what some ancients call the ages of humanity. And even the nomads, or the very old ones who lived in small settlements had some temple or rock or stone circle to connect with the divine. And then we have the stories, and the drawings of the angels, the winged beings of fire and light who appear in their many forms all over the place, both in terms of spatial location, and chronology. Now the angels it would seem, are only seen on extraordinary occasions, usually when something important is about to happen. And when they do appear, people do see them,' said Andri.

'And? Some believe there are no angels, only aliens, UFOs, other beings from other planets who are more evolved than us, and come here to study us, or to help. That could also explain any sightings of "angels" so to speak!' Kevin, a 'retired' pagan who didn't much believe in any of it anyway, and who loved a good mindbender, was playing devils advocate.

'Ah, yes. Many possibilities there as well!' said Andri. 'No doubt in my mind anyway, that both exist. The aliens, well, considering the countless number of stars, and therefore also the huge potential number of planets harbouring some form of life, it would be very arrogant and quite blind of us to assume there are no aliens more advanced than us, and having the technology to travel to our Earth, to observe and learn. However, given this potential, why don't they just land in Central Park, NY, and introduce themselves? Give us some of that good technology and some hints on life and so on? If they are enlightened, why don't they share? If not enlightened, but nasty, how come they don't gobble us up or something? I think that the answer is the same one to the question of if there is an afterlife, how come no one's come back to tell us? It has to do with not being allowed to interfere. Letting things develop as they will, letting us as beings, as a planetary existence have the freedom to be. The freedom of will. But then again ... I just saw the hole in that one. If we are protected from other beings, then how come were not protected from each other?'

'One race, nation subjugates another, here on Earth we call that history!' Kevin was having a good old time, this time he didn't even have to argue it out.

'There must be safeguards. Could you imagine what it would be like if there were none? Ghosts haunting their killers, people killing themselves just to join a loved one who has "departed", if things were really nice on the other side, or imagine how horrified we would be if all we could see is hell awaiting us!' Andri was trying to revive his thoughts, always an optimist that rationality could and would show the way when intuition was asleep.

'There is of course the very real possibility that there is no life after death, no angels or aliens, just this, here and now!' Kevin was in his element here, a cynic to the max, yet deeply spiritual, he loved to bring down any half baked notions but not as much as moving to the core of the story. 'That would explain why no one ever comes back after dying to tell us about it. It's all here and in a fleeting moment it's gone. But I suspect we've veered off here, what about the ancient civilisations and all that?'

'Yes, well, it's the stories about the Guardians ... I keep

seeing them.' Andri went quiet and lowered his head. 'I shouldn't have said that ...' he thought to himself. He knew that he had just set himself up for questioning, and disappointment. Sure enough, Kevin was right on it.

'You take a massive dose of acid and you see angels. Why am I not surprised? I'll tell you why, because I've heard the story so many times, from so many different people .... .The things people see, well it's all real at some level, symbolic at another, but then again you can get too far away from reality if you live in an altered state of mind for too long ...' Kevin was taking the soft approach to bringing his friend back to earth. He himself had been to the edge a few times, peering over the fathomless void. He was older though, and felt some responsibility for his younger friends, seeing them discover those special places he already knew well.

'Yeah man, you know the pitfalls. The halfway houses are full of people who went too far too fast!' said Nash from the corner of the room.

'You should talk!' argued Thodoras in defence of his friend, who seemed to be on the ropes all of a sudden. 'I've seen you take massive doses, so don't you start preaching now!'

'Well, yes, but it doesn't affect me in that way. I don't get visions, just a good time, you know ...' Nash's apologetic tone did nothing to change things. Andri had taken on the assault on himself, internally. He respected Kevin, and although he didn't always agree with his views he always heard what he had to say, and considered it carefully. His mind had latched onto the loss of perspective idea and was milling it around whilst the conversation, which continued without him, faded away as if it was happening somewhere else. He focused on his perception of himself, and how that was somehow pivotal to his perception of everything else. Basically he considered himself common as muck. That wasn't a put down on himself, quite the contrary, he saw it as an achievement and honour. All the real people he knew and loved so much were common, like him, no matter what they thought of themselves or whether they were more or less 'intelligent' – whatever that may be. Intelligence takes so many forms, how could you know? So far as Andri was concerned intelligence had more to do with walking the path, being, unfolding. The rest was social boxes designed mainly to help the big companies chose their employees efficiently. Differences between people were like drawings on the white sheet of similarities. Some used grey lead pencils, others all the colours of the rainbow. He'd like to think he used many colours in his life, but did he?

'Hmm, yes I know the one. Green eyes, average height, soft brown flowing hair, and a sizzling body, I remember her dancing . . .' Andri listened to Thodoras just enough to realise that in his absence the conversation had changed subject to something more earthly. He smiled and tuned out again. Know yourself. How was he different, what was his drawing like? In all respects he was just like everyone else, he thought, apart maybe from one thing. The visions. Here he felt quite alone. It wasn't that others didn't have visions, many surely had, although it took some effort to discern what was true and what was made up by either well wishing eagerness or calculated fraud; it didn't matter, the result was ultimately the same – misinformation, more illusion building. Surely there were others, but he hadn't met any himself. He had read the many prophetic visions of various holy people throughout the ages, and some of his contemporaries, but he'd never met any of them. The visions made him different. But why give them to him? 'The Great Spirit obviously loves laughter and humour.' The thought just seemed to pop into his mind. It felt reassuringly like a loose end in this tangled web. He followed it. The white robed purists he so despised in a way were coming back to haunt him. Why not pick one of them? They'd have no problem accepting that role, and the message would surely be forthcoming from such eloquent mouths! The drawback of course would be that people wouldn't believe them lot, not the down to earth people, and that mattered. But then again nobody seemed to believe him either, not even his friends. Even at the rainbow he'd soon abandoned the idea of talking to anyone about his experiences, and chose to stay quiet. What chance did he have now in the city?

No, Kevin was right to criticise him, to point out the obvious, that he was in danger of losing touch with reality. He had no outlet for his visions, and he wasn't likely to forget them, so maybe he should push them to the back of his mind and focus more on the now. There was always more to know, more inner barriers to overcome, more growing up to undergo. And the visions could be a distraction, keeping him from doing all that he needs to in order to change, to evolve.

CHAPTER 15

A BRIDGE TO THE SKY

As we stand on grandmother earth, raising our sacred pipe in prayer, its stem forms a bridge from earth through man through our own bodies, to the sky, to Wakan Tanka, the grandfather spirit. As the pipe is filled with our sacred red willow bark tobacco, each tiny grain represents one of the living things on this earth. All of the Great Spirit's creations, the whole universe, is in that pipe. All of us in that pipe at the moment of prayer. Often we are so overwhelmed by this that we cry and burst into tears as we raise the pipe towards the clouds.[2]

-JOHN FIRE LAME DEER-

The seasons were changing, and so was the world around Andri. 'The Seeds' would soon disperse, each taking on their own path, but now their paths diverged leading them far from each other. What had brought them together had ended, and the notorious change of season parties were soon but a distant memory of the 'good old days'. The rehashing of those memories even became yesterday's news after a period of lingering get-togethers. Going around one more time the loop of life Andri found himself once again at that place where he had lost his friends. By now it felt almost welcome, like a familiar landmark, a park bench to sit alone for a while on the way home.

Ever since the Spring Street days he worked hard to fit in. Brick by brick he erected the mental structures, the excuses, and justifications that would keep him isolated from his visions. He'd had enough of being a misfit and made an effort to become a 'responsible member of society' even if he disagreed with most that was going on anyway. His deeper feelings he covered under the cloak of oblivion, and hid his anger under a carpet of sarcasm and bitterness. He had convinced himself that to sacrifice his life for others was the responsible thing to do, but as he placed himself in increasingly unfriendly environments he soon limited his responsibility to his immediate family, to the exclusion of much else. It was a nasty and unfriendly world out there and it wasn't getting any better. The peace sign in the sky was no more on his mind, just bitter-sweet memories of hippie gatherings in the woods, a sense of a bubble burst, a dream eroded, lost.

Life in the mainstream provides ample distractions for those running away from themselves. Big arms stretch out of the television screen and massage your brain in between the bad news bulletin and the late night violent film. The big life of small things takes over. The absence of real satisfaction is brushed aside by the carrot on the stick of rewards later in life, which requires an investment of time and effort. And life goes on, in pursuit of a hazy dream, which we soon chose to forget. Andri was lost, asleep. Occasionally, some memory would come knocking on the door, some remnant from his psychedelic past like snippets from a Talking Heads song: "And you will ask yourself: my God, what have I done? ... Same at it ever was, same as it ever was ... water running underground ..." but he'd brush it aside and laugh at himself.

Yet the wheel of life stops for no one and like the untruths in his mind his false balance was exposed by his own life's circumstances. If life was a boat, his had certainly capsized. All the dissatisfaction and suppressed feelings inside him ended up making a big mirror and showing him this truth about himself. That he had lost his way. Anyone could do most of the things he occupied himself with routinely, and so he realised he had reached a point where he had nothing to give. He had managed to neglect himself so consistently and truly that he was empty, a mere shell of a person – a body housing a potential.

The age old questions came back to nudge him. What was he there for? What was the purpose of his existence?

Everything had become hazy in his mind. Nothing seemed well defined any more, and he felt as if he was walking around aimlessly in the fog yet again. 'This is alright, I've been here before and I know that eventually things will clear out.' He thought out loud. Speaking the words, hearing them from outside as well as from inside was the pivotal point he was expecting, he recognised the turning place – a feeling of power awakening. Yet, this time something was different. It felt something like the body memory that comes from repeated actions, like tying a knot without thinking about it. His hands led him to his small travelling bag, the one he always took with him. Inside, amongst a variety of papers and stones was something made of black wool. He pulled it out. It was a prayer hoop, a series of knots with a cross formed out of the wool itself on the one end and a blue bead opposite from it. Andri started feeling the knots, casting his mind back to that visit of the monasteries up North, where the prayer rope was made. The monks would go through a short prayer as they tied each knot, tying together awareness and purpose, and using the material itself to hold that energy manifest. He never doubted its alchemical value.

Andri let himself take a deep breath, asking himself what his prayer was. He didn't have to go far inside to find the answer, and as soon as it flashed in his mind it was also on his lips: 'To learn the lesson so I don't get so lost again!' This time he was determined. He wasn't going to let go of the opportunity to learn the lesson, to overcome his boundaries, to heal and grow. He felt like a dog with a bone between his teeth, jaw locked. Systematically he gathered his old notes, pictures and things from the past and started going through them, looking for clues, trying to feel for the end of that thread he was once working on, his life. He still believed, he realised from his old notes, that it's all in the childhood. Somewhere in there in those first years, all was played out symbolically, for our own benefit. Everything we need in order to grow to our true potential lies in those experiences, empowered by innocence and the feeling – the memory of where we came from and to what end. Like children ... only there was nothing stopping us from being like children again, innocence might have been lost but what is to say it can't be re-gained? The thought gathered momentum in his head like a brewing storm out in the vast ocean. He grabbed onto his early memories and started pulling.

The more he started remembering how he was a few years ago, the more it became clear to Andri that to see the truth one had to be like a child, free from preconceptions, open to the endless possibilities manifesting in the universe. For in his old writing there was a lot that made him smile, from romantic expressions of 'love' to explorations on the edge of the mind, but also, every now and then something intriguing, an inkling of a clue, a lose thread of light dangling in his consciousness.

'Voices from the depths of eternity
I hear them
Waves from the beginning of creation
I feel them'

He prayed, opening his heart to the trust that the universe would provide what he needed. He prayed for the strength to accept the truth about his life, to forgive himself, to accept himself and then to give himself to its higher purpose. He prayed for the strength to let go of all his preconceptions about life, to be able to see with the eyes of a child once again.

This time, to know himself he had to go deeper, further back. He was ready for the barriers, or so he thought because it was only pain he considered he would find there, when in fact it was joy as well. He never thought of joy as a barrier, he never even suspected that he would have problems feeling joy. And yet, some aspect of his being was for ever denying him the deep feeling of joy, as if he didn't deserve it. It took Andri a long time to overcome this, to break that part of the illusion. He kept on arguing to himself that if pain and suffering need to be experienced to be transcended, then so should joy need to be experienced and overcome. His mind kept on pounding at the door, and his heart searched for the guidance of the divine female, the goddess within. Time was now of little essence and his inner search had taken by now the form of a full grown stag tearing through the forest of his life experiences, shaking the debris of leaves from his antlers, stomping his hooves on the dense forest floor. A soft, calming light, glowing somewhere on his left, elusive and yet present guided him to the small clearing where he saw her. She was standing taller than life, dressed in deer skin, moonlight shimmering around her and inside a warm light like the myriad red brown and gold hues of the autumn leaves. His heart knew her but he found himself asking: 'What is your name, beloved?' 'I am a tear in your eyes,' she replied and stroked the side of his head. Golden light came through her fingers and into his skull. He felt the heat go through what must have been an old wound and instinctively he raised his hand to his head. His skull felt strange, a very intense and specific feeling, one he'd felt before. 'I've been shown something,' he muttered to himself, and he closed his eyes again to try and trace that feeling. It didn't take long for him to find it. It was the feeling he got when he held the monk's skull, back on the island many years ago. He was overtaken by a childish enthusiasm, pacing up and down his room, focusing on the travelling bag. 'The game's afoot Watson!' he declared to himself almost laughing at the same time. He was alive, not only because of the prospect of the journey, but more so for the feeling that years of work were coming to fruition.

A few weeks later he was travelling, following his intuition. It had been a long time since he had done something like this, pursuing a hazy dream, a vision given in a moment, a glimpse of a feeling, and a question mark. The port had seemed almost welcoming, in spite of the wintry starkness and urban grime. Maybe it was the seagulls, the smell of stormy weather, air filled with salty sea spray. Andri found a comfortable spot in the not so busy old ferry. It was a five hour journey in fair weather, and he hadn't slept much the night before as he was catching up with old friends. The rhythmic humming of the big engine followed the pattern of the waves as the propeller took on more or less strain. He soon fell asleep.

In his dream, Andri found himself in the woods. He was up on a big old oak tree, lying on one of the big lower branches with his stomach touching the moist bark. As he looked down he saw a boy nestled between the big roots and the tree trunk. The boy stirred as he dreamed. Andri recognised the boy, it was him. Although he didn't look like what Andri used to look like when he was a boy, it was still undeniably himself he was looking at, and he was dreaming. He wondered what the little boy was dreaming of, and instantly he felt as if he was falling into the abyss.

The little boy opened his eyes. His dream was so vivid that he could remember every detail. He dreamed that he was in the jungle at night, stomping around when he saw a light. Someone had a fire somewhere close by, and he was cold and tired so he decided to go there. It led him to the entrance of a small cave. The fire was warm and there was no trace of anyone about so he sat by it. Suddenly he realised he wasn't alone. Sitting by the fire were four animal spirits. He recognised them as spirits because they also looked like people and there was a shimmering light around their form. The first one to speak was the Raven.

'I will always be there for you, I will sing songs for your heart to hear, songs from the beginning and the end. Whispers they may sound to your ears until you open your heart to the music, to the sacred sounds from the eternal void from which all emerged. Then you will hear the messages I carry and you will know I have been next to you all along.'

Then spoke the Lizard: 'I will warm your bones and soul. I will show you how to remember, how to understand and talk with the old ones, the rock people. I will teach you how to walk over the bridge of fire; to see the powers that lie within the pools of molten rock. The light you cannot contain . . .'

The Bear spoke next: 'You can always rely on my strength. I will protect you from the illusion, I will help you to clear the path to your power. I will help you in your long journey to discover past and future memories, to accept who you are.'

Last spoke the black Jaguar: 'I will release you from the burden of your ego; to me you can surrender and I will take you to many places of power. I will be with you in the beginning and the end. When I come to you the second time, it will be a time of great change in this world. Look for me then in your dream of dreams.'

The little boy peered through his half open eyelids. It was still dark in the deep forest. The sweet smell of sleep was still around him. He turned and shut his eyes. Soon he was asleep again, and Andri was again watching himself dream. He opened his eyes suddenly, startled by the sharp pounding sound of the heavy steel chain against the ships anchor housing. He scrambled to get down to the lower deck and off the boat; ferries didn't hang about for dreamers.

The short taxi ride to the village kept him distracted. The quick conversation with the driver on benefits of diesel engines was enough to ground Andri in the temporary world of little things. The effects lasted just long enough for him to get into his grandmother's house and make himself a warm cup of coffee. The summer had long ended and there was an autumnal dampness in the air. The house had been shut for a while as it was infrequently used now that the spirited old woman was gone. An old electric radiator was potentially the only source of heat, but it looked too old to be safe, and it would likely blow the house fuse. He decided to open the shutters and take advantage of the warming rays of grandfather Sun. There where still a few hours of daylight left, but he was so anxious that as soon as he warmed up a bit he was out again, and on the dirt path leading out of the back of the village and towards the ruins of the Byzantine monastery. He was there within an hour, his heart pounding hard in his chest, looking around in the receding sunlight for that one boulder ... the thought that he might not find the skull even, let alone anything else, teased on the edge of his mind. He started sweating. 'Breathe!' he told himself, putting his right hand over his chest. He turned and tripped, almost spraining his ankle, and sat on the ground holding his leg. As he shut his eyes he took a deep breath, and leaned back on a boulder. He breathed a bit more, deliberately slow deep breaths, placing his hands on the ground by his hips. His right hand slipped through a hole, and without even turning he knew he'd found it. He sprang up and started prodding with his hands in the hole under the boulder. He felt the skull and carefully lifted it out, reliving the first moment he touched it. His whole body shook as if he was holding on to a lingering branch over a fiercely rapid river. He placed it safely on the ground and kept on feeling his way through. Underneath the small twigs that formed like a nest for the skull he could feel something different, it felt more like ... leather! Carefully he pulled out what looked like some animal hide, leather and fur, a sort of bundle all wrapped up.

Andri unwrapped it slowly, realising that the contents had not seen the Sun's light since the time of the monk's death, surely a few hundred years. As he unwrapped it he noted that it was an unusual type of leather, surely not cow, but something inside told him it was actually bear, although that surely didn't make any sense. He finally opened the fourth and last layer. Inside was a stone pipe, with a wooden stem. The wood was so old it almost immediately crumbled as he tried to handle it. He recognised the red stone bowl immediately as a Native American tribal pipe. 'A medicine pipe!' he quietly exclaimed to no-one around. He sat on the ground holding the red stone bowl in his hands, by his heart. He closed his eyes and drifted. As soon as he could quiet his mind it jumped out at him. The vision startled him so much that he almost fell over. He saw a mountainside of red clay, out of which protruded the wailing faces of all the mothers whose children were massacred. He opened his eyes but he could still hear the crying. He cried and cried through the sunset. It was dark by the time he'd put the skull back. The pipe he took, as he felt straight away the connection, he felt- he knew- that he had held it before.

☯

Weeks later, after a series of dreams having to do with the pipe, he started carving out a wooden stem for it. The process had now begun, and as he started realising more and more the significance and power of it, it became a sacred tool once again. And as time went by and Andri started using the sacred pipe to pray to the Great Spirit, his inner wounds began to heal and he slowly remembered more and more of the past. The dreams, the visions, all started making sense to him, revealing more and more of what his journey had been. As he always suspected it was all in a nutshell represented in the childhood, even if it was only in the some hidden part of play, away from other eyes. His heart was opening up, accepting the memories, trusting deep down inside that the universe will provide what is needed, that all will work out in the end. Life after life, time an time again, he chased the unifying thread, the core of his being. Soon he started realising the patterns were there.

Bear spirit led him deeper and deeper into his cave of dreams and more detail came flooding through. John, Esme, Guisepe . . . the Ghostdance! His heart followed the thread across the big seas to the turtle continent.

He felt home once again. Like with the rainbow gathering, it was a feeling of belonging, of deep knowing of a place. Many dreams, many visions. With the eyes of a child, held back by an elder, he could see as the white soldiers massacred his people. Bear medicine had helped him survive that one. That kind of medicine had been known to him from much earlier on he felt. Much further back, into his childhood of existence he dragged himself through the trail of tears. On the way he encountered much help, from the Elders, the Ancient ones, the Guardians, and his old friends, who he started to discover where largely present in this lifetime. And although it had often occurred in some conversation or other that there was a mutual feeling of having known each other before, it was almost always a very nebulous feeling with no specific memories attached. Now, he realised, he could actually remember detailed events of the past, and he thought it must be just a matter of time before others do too if they aren't already. It was all quite a lot to take in, but bit by bit he persisted, and help was always there for him, so he kept going.

☯

Again his life had changed in the process; he was becoming the weird one, more marginalised as a mainstream character, and more real, more alive than ever. Peeling away the layers of the ego, until there was nothing more or less than experience itself took time and like every journey had its stops and diversions, mostly to do with learning to be again, at a different level, developing his inner strengths. He remembered being on top of a hill, his people lying dead in the valleys below, massacred by those who didn't want to see. He saw himself, an old man, torn to pieces by grief, looking at the stars and asking 'How much longer?' and it took him months to even try going back again. And yet he came back, and asked the same question of his core, his essence. 'Who am I really?' and he pulled, to the child, the child he'd seen in his dreams many times before, the child in the jungle.

Until one night, offering the sacred pipe in prayer under the starry sky he heard his name and knew at once who he really was, and why he was remembering it all. Aeeneean looked the stars. He raised the pipe to the sky offering his prayer of gratitude. The white smoke spiralled up towards the stars dancing on the thin mountain air.

Inside his heart the earth drum made its deep, rhythmic presence known. Rising up from the soles of his feet he could feel the warmth of mother Earth's love. His body started shaking, becoming a bridge to the sky. Starlight streamed through the top of his head and down his spine on its way to the Earth's centre.

Aeeneean held the pipe to his heart and from deep inside released his voice like a wild horse.

'I AM still here Great Spirit!'

A tear of joy and a tear of sorrow trickled from his eyes, merging together and dropping as one onto the Earth. 'Soon my friends,' he whispered, 'soon we'll be free.'

REFERENCES

1. Steinmetz, Paul B (2001), *Meditations with the Lakota*, Bear and Co., Rochester, Vermont.
2. John (Fire) Lame Deer and Richard Erdoes (1972), *Lame Deer, Seeker of Visions*, Simon & Schuster, Inc., New York, NY.

Printed in the United Kingdom
by Lightning Source UK Ltd.
124484UK00001B/193-213/A